INSIGHT POCKET GUIDE

APA PUBLICATIONS L

Part of the Langenscheidt Publishing Group

Malta and the Central Mediterranen

240 km / 150 miles

Welcome!

This guidebook combines the interests and enthusiasms of two of the world's best-known information providers: Insight Guides, who have set the standard for visual travel guides since 1970, and Discovery Channel, the world's premier source of non-fiction television programming.

Insight Guides' expert on Malta has captured the best of these fascinating islands, located at the crossroads of three continents. A selection of carefully crafted itineraries, designed to suit a variety of tastes and time frames, includes full-day walking tours around Valletta, Mdina and Rabat, cities rich in Arab and Crusader history; several coastal hikes; drives into the interior for ruins and crafts; and two full-day options on Malta's twin island of Gozo, just a 25-minute ferry ride away. But it isn't all sightseeing and history – the book also points out the best coves for swimming, the places to sample Maltese cuisine and when to experience Malta's *festas*.

Lyle Lawson is a long-term devotee of Malta. Her work as a freelance writer and photographer takes her back time and time again. She has scanned the terrain from a helicopter, descended into the depths of Ghar Hasan, hiked most of the southern coastline, won and lost money at the casino and has photographed more baroque churches on Malta than she can remember. In this book her main aim has been to show the diversity of Malta and the Maltese, a people whom she finds 'ebullient and very warm-hearted', characteristics that reflect their outgoing, seafaring history.

C O N T E N T S

History & Culture

Carthaginian naval base, Arab outpost, headquarters of the Knights of St John, a British Crown colony – a brief account of landmark events in Malta's history **10**

Malta's Highlights

Two full-day itineraries explore the main cities of Malta: the Knights' city of Valletta and the twin cities of Mdina and Rabat. They include stops for refreshment and relaxation en route.

Day 1 concentrates on the historic centre of *Valletta*, in particular *St John's Co-Cathedral* and the *Palace of the Knights*. After lunch, the route circles the bastions for far-reaching views **20**

Day 2 focuses on medieval *Mdina* and its 'suburb' *Rabat*. Highlights include a Roman villa, early Christian catacombs, dungeons and Mdina's sublime cathedral. The day ends with a cruise around the *Grand Harbour* **29**

Pick & Mix Itineraries

1. A Central Circle begins with a tour of *San Anton Palace and Gardens* and a visit to the *Ta 'Qali Crafts Centre*. It then proceeds to *Mosta* and *Birkirkara* for impressive churches **36**

2. The Three Cities explores *Senglea*, *Cospicua* and *Vittoriosa*...**39**

3 The Southeast combines prehistoric ruins, fishing villages and swimming at *Peter's Pool*. Alternative routes for drivers and walkers are supplied..........**44**

4. Quarries and Temples begins with a visit to a quarry, then takes a boat ride through the *Blue Grotto* and visits the prehistoric temples of *Hagar Qim* and *Mnajdra*...**47**

5. The South Coast visits *Verdala Palace* and *Buskett Gardens* and takes a walk along *Dingli Cliffs*............**48**

6. Exploring Malta's Tail combines a visit to the shrine of *St Mary of Mellieha* and Malta's most popular beach **50**

7. A Night on the Town highlights the best nightlife **52**

Pages 2/3:
Valletta and St
Julian's from the air

Gozo's Highlights

A full-day itinerary highlighting the main sights of Gozo, Malta's smaller neighbour, has been designed for visitors on a day-trip from Malta. For those with more time in Gozo, this is followed by two further options.

Day 1 is a walk through Gozo's capital, *Victoria*, concentrating on the *Citadel*. Afterwards, it suggests a visit to *Ggantija*, a prehistoric temple **55**

Option 1. A Ring Around the Island is a drive around Gozo's coastline, taking in churches, beaches, fishing harbours, a glass-blowing centre and the *Azure Window*, a natural rock formation **60**

Option 2. Cruise to Comino and the Blue Lagoon is a boat trip to the tiny isle of *Comino* which lies in between Malta and Gozo. It suggests a walk from *Santa Marija Bay* and swimming in the clear waters of the *Blue Lagoon* **65**

Excursions

A selection of excursions, including exploring the seabed by submarine and touring the Three Cities by 1920s bus **66**

Shopping & Eating Out

Tips on what to buy and advice on where to eat..............**68–75**

Calendar of Special Events

A detailed list of Malta's main festivals **76–7**

Practical Information

All the background information you will need for your stay, including a discriminating list of hotels.................**78–91**

Maps

Malta and the Central	**The Three Cities**.................**39**
Mediterranean **4**	**South East Malta** **44**
The Maltese Islands....**18–19**	**Malta's Tail** **50**
Valletta..................................**20**	**Victoria**................................**57**
Mdina and Rabat................**29**	**Gozo**.....................................**60**
A Central Circle.................**36**	

Index and Credits 92–4

Pages 8/9: traditional boat design

Lying almost dead centre in the Mediterranean, 58 miles (93km) due south of Sicily, 220 miles (352km) north of Libya, with Tunisia 180 miles (288km) to the west and with Syria and Lebanon the first land to the east, Malta's geographical position has often determined the course of its history. The island is either a hindrance or a sentinel depending upon the perspective from which it is regarded.

The Cross and the Crescent

The temples of Mnajdra on Gozo and Hagar Qim on Malta bear witness to a flourishing civilisation during the early Bronze Age (c. 3500BC) but after that little is known of Malta's history until the 4th century BC when the Greeks were supreme in the eastern part of the Mediterranean, and Carthage ruled the west. In the middle stood Malta.

During the Third Punic War, Malta's Grand Harbour became a Carthaginian naval base; when Carthage lost the war, Malta was given to the Romans, who generally ignored the island. Around AD60, however, a ship was caught by the rocks off the northwestern

The Grand Harbour, first established by the Carthaginians

Culture

The temple of Mnajdra

coast of Malta. According to legend, St Paul was on board, being taken to Rome for trial. He has been credited with laying the foundations for the strong faith for which the Maltese are still known. Publius, the Roman governor of the island, was an early convert, and by the 3rd century most islanders were Christians.

After the fall of Rome, Malta experienced a period of relative peace. Even the arrival of the Arabs in 870 was almost a non-event; they came, conquered quickly, and ruled benignly, leaving behind a major legacy, their language, which forms the basis for much of *il Malti*, the Maltese language.

Count Roger the Norman, whose stronghold was on Sicily, conquered Malta in 1091 and, for the next several hundred years, whoever was ruling Sicily also ruled Malta. In the 1400s Malta became part of the domain of Ferdinand of Aragon and Isabella of Castile, the 'Catholic monarchs', but was not confirmed as a Christian country until 1565, when the Knights of St John of Jerusalem (or Knights Hospitallers) vanquished the Infidel (the Arabs).

Founded in 1085, the Order's original purpose was to care for pilgrims who fell ill on visits to the Holy Land. But when Godfrey de Bouillon, a leader of the first Crusade, captured Jerusalem in 1099 their role began to change. By the time the Order was placed under papal protection in 1113, the Knights had become fighters, although they still protected and treated pilgrims.

After Jerusalem fell to Islam in 1187, Richard the Lionheart moved the Order to Acre; when Sultan Kahil took that city in 1291, the Knights had to move again – to Cyprus. Rhodes became the Order's new home in 1310, and for over 200 years they fought, and beat, the Turks in the eastern Mediterranean. Their power seemed invincible and their fortress island impregnable. No Ottoman Sultan was able to take the heavily defended island until the advent of Suleiman, known as 'The Magnificent', and considered the greatest of the Ottoman Sultans.

In June 1522 Suleiman attacked Rhodes. Six months later, he allowed the Knights to leave Rhodes with their

Symbol in silver

The Great Siege of 1565, a fresco from the Palace of the Knights

honour intact and they began searching for a permanent home.

Seven years later, Charles V, grandson of Ferdinand and Isabella, offered the Knights of St John a home in Malta, where they made Birgu (later named Vittoriosa) their base. The Maltese people, as usual, had no say about their island being given to outsiders but the Knights were welcomed as defenders against the Barbary Coast corsairs, who were regularly raiding and looting Malta and its sister island Gozo, taking slaves and hostages.

In 1565 an Ottoman fleet of 181 ships sailed from Constantinople carrying a complement of over 30,000 men. Their mission was simple: destroy everything Christian and redeem the Mediterranean for Allah. On 18 May the Turkish ships sailed into view of Malta and unexpectedly launched an attack on Fort St Elmo. The Knights held firm, despite being the target of over 7,000 rounds of ammunition every day; nevertheless, on 23 June the Turks raised their flag over the fort. Fewer than a dozen Maltese survived, but the Turkish loss was also massive. The assault on the island continued and on 7 August the walls of Birgu were breached and Turkish victory seemed to be assured. But the Knights continued to resist, and when word arrived of reinforcements from Sicily the Turks retreated, and shortly after left the islands altogether. The following day, 8 September, the Great Siege was over and the Knights' cross was once again flying over the bastions of St Elmo. Those whom Sulieman the Magnificent had spared on Rhodes had lived to defeat his legions on Malta.

The Knights Have Their Day

Grand Master Jean Parisot de la Valette, the Knights' leader, was declared the saviour of Christendom, and Birgu and Senglea were renamed Vittoriosa and Invicta. But the toll had been high: 220

Knights dead, a further 9,000 soldiers slain, countless wounded and the island's fortifications shattered.

The Grand Master decided that a new capital was needed, and Mount Sceberras, behind Fort St Elmo, was chosen. The architect was Francesco Laparelli, an assistant to Michelangelo, and in 1566 Valletta, named after the hero of the Siege, was inaugurated.

In 1568, the Maltese architect and engineer Gerolamo Cassar was put in charge of building the city, and it is his work that we see today. One of his major projects included accommodation for the Eight Langues, or languages, into which the Knights were grouped, representing Germany, Italy, Castile, Aragon, Provence, Auvergne, France and England. However, now that destruction by the forces of Islam was no longer an imminent threat, the Knights began to forget their vows of poverty, chastity and humility. The simple auberges of Vittoriosa were replaced by larger, more elaborate ones; rich food and fine wines were consumed; elegant robes of silk and brocade were worn instead of chain-mail; and mistresses were openly flaunted. Worse, however, was the rebirth of piracy, taken up not against the Islamic infidel but against fellow Christians.

When revolution erupted in France in 1789, many of the French Knights joined Condé's Royalist army of Rebellion or donated money to Louis XVI. In 1791 they were deprived of their nationality and a year later the Order's estates and revenues in France were confiscated. Deprived of their French revenues, the Knights looked for another source of income. The Russian Tsar Paul I offered to found an Orthodox Langue and assume the title of Protector of the Order. However the British, wishing to keep both Russia and the French out of the Mediterranean, initiated their own talks with the then Grand Master de Rohan-Polduc but in 1797, before the negotiations could be completed, he died.

The new Grand Master, Ferdinand de Hompesch, accepted the Russian offer. This particularly enraged Napoleon and, leaving Italy which he had just conquered, he made anchor outside the Grand Harbour in June 1798. When he was refused entry, he opened fire. After two days of shelling, the French landed and gave the Knights four days to leave, thus ending their 268-year presence on Malta.

No one was sorry to see them go; the Maltese rejoiced and lit bonfires, the French troops looted the Knights' auberges and palaces and Napoleon had their hospital's silver-service melted down to pay for his troops' expenses in Egypt before sailing off to his disastrous encounter with Lord Nelson.

After Napoleon's departure,

Ferdinand de Hompesch

British crest

the French troops became even more ruthless. Provoked, the Maltese eventually responded by massacring the French garrison at Mdina. The French commander retreated to Valletta, and waited in vain for help from Napoleon. A blockade of Valletta's land approaches was set up by the locals, and a Portuguese fleet, aided later by a British squadron, stood at the harbour entrance to protect the island against the return of Napoleon. The French force finally capitulated in 1800.

Maltese citizens were adamant that they did not want a return of either the French or the Knights. Britain, which had by now ruled fairly for two years, was preferable to both. In 1814 Russia, no longer allied with France, formally renounced any intention of helping the Knights regain their position in Malta. The islands were formally made a British Crown Colony, and became one of the Empire's most loyal possessions, adopting the English language and law and becoming an important stop on the route from Britain to India. During World War I more than 25,000 casualties were taken to Malta for treatment.

In 1921 the first self-governing constitution was granted. This left Britain in control of immigration and foreign policy and the Maltese responsible for domestic affairs. The 1930s saw a series of disagreements between the British Governor General, the church and local politicians, and although the internal conflicts were resolved by 1936, an even greater external one was brewing.

Valletta in World War II

GREAT SIEGE
· ROAD
TRIQ
L-ASSEDJU L-KBIR

The Invincible Islands

As the Fascist party in Italy strengthened, so did Mussolini's designs on Malta. On 10 June 1940, he declared war against the Allied powers. The following day the first bombing raids on Malta began.

Malta was an impressive target and a vulnerable one: there were 30,000 British and Maltese troops on the island and a civilian population of around 250,000. The dry docks were among the most modern in Europe. Many politicians in London wanted to evacuate and let Mussolini have his way, but Churchill, convinced of Malta's long-term strategic importance, prevailed. The islands defended themselves, the people burrowing into air-raid shelters by day and night as the Italian planes dropped their lethal cargoes. By November the number of raids had reached almost 200, with scarcely a return run on the Italian bases on Sicily. In 1941, with Mussolini's air force no closer to capturing Malta despite air supremacy, the German Luftwaffe entered the battle. They had one aim: to cut the island's supply lines. Without engine fuel, spare parts, oil and food, the islanders would have no choice but to surrender. In early 1941 a decision by Rommel to concentrate on Tobruk gave the island a respite, but the relative peace was not to last. Before the Germans could secure North Africa they had to neutralise Malta; and if Malta would not surrender then it could starve.

In January 1942, the island's second Great Siege commenced and continued through March and April. Twice as many bombs fell on Malta as fell on London in a whole year at the height of London's Blitz. Buildings were flattened, 40,000 homes were destroyed and the islands were completely blockaded.

On 15 April 1942, King George VI awarded the islands the George Cross. The citation reads: 'To honour a brave people I award the George Cross to the island fortress of Malta to bear witness to a heroism and a devotion that will long be famous in history.' By mid-May Malta had less than three months' supply of food, and if help did not arrive soon, the island would have to surrender. Fortunately a convoy was on its way, guarded by an extraordinary number of battleships, aircraft carriers, cruisers and destroyers. Many were lost en route but on 13 August *Port Chalmers*, *Melbourne Star* and *Rochester Castle* reached port, followed by the *Brisbane Star* and the tanker *Ohio*, carrying much-needed aviation fuel.

Thereafter the German concentration on North Africa lessened the pressure on Malta. In January 1943 the Allies took Tripoli and in May Germany's Afrika Korps, denied their means of escape

Malta's George Cross

across the Mediterranean by the tenacity of the Maltese, were taken prisoner.

General Eisenhower sent the Maltese a message: 'The epic of Malta is symbolic of the experience of the United Nations in this war; Malta has passed successively through the stages of woeful unpreparedness, tenacious endurance, intensive preparation and the initiation of a fierce offensive.' In May 1943, King George VI made a surprise visit to thank the island. In July, the invasion of Sicily was launched from Malta, and on 8 September the Italian fleet surrendered. Malta had survived its second Great Siege.

Malta Goes It Alone

After World War II there were many cries for independence, or pleas at least to become part of the UK with proper representation in the House of Commons. A referendum was

Freedom Day celebrates independence

easily passed, but less than two-thirds of the population voted, and the British thereafter voided the result. Dom Mintoff, a republican and socialist prime minister (three times between 1971 and 1984) ruffled feathers when he forged alliances with socialist countries. Several turbulent years followed as Mintoff battled with Whitehall. On 21 September 1964 independence within the Commonwealth was granted, and on 13 December 1974, Malta was declared a republic. The last British base closed in 1979.

Today Malta is a self-governing republic with a prime minister as leader of the government and a parliament of 65 members; the role of president is ceremonial. Malta has been a member of the Council of Europe since 1964. Under the Labour Party it froze its application to join the EU in 1996, but the Nationalists reinstated it in 1998.

Tourism is one of the main sources of foreign currency today, as are the revitalised dockyards which have an international reputation for the repair of liners and tankers. High technology is a priority in education.

The Maltese are convinced that just as they have withstood two major sieges during their history, they can face the 21st century with the confidence of true survivors.

Signs of the times

Historical Highlights

Pre-5 million BC Malta is part of land mass joining Europe to Africa.

5000 Neolithic Age; Red and Grey Skorba period; temple of Ta'Hagrat built.

4000–3000 The Copper Age; megalithic temples built at Ggantija, Tarxien, Hagar Qim and Mnajdra.

2500–900 The Bronze Age; Borg in-Nadur inhabited.

675–600 Phoenician colonisation.

480 Carthaginian domination.

264 First Punic War.

218 Malta incorporated into Republic of Rome.

AD**60** St Paul shipwrecked, and converts Publius to Christianity.

330 Byzantine rule begins.

533 Belisarius, Justinian's great general, makes port on Malta.

870 The Aghlabid Caliphs conquer the island, bringing their language which forms the basis for *il Malti*.

1091 The Normans land; Count Roger of Sicily's Christian force routs the Arabs.

1266–83 Angevin dynasty rules.

1283–1530 The Spanish Aragonese on Malta.

1350 King Ludwig of Sicily establishes the Maltese nobility.

1530 The Order of St John takes possession of the islands.

1551 Gozo attacked by Ottoman forces. After prolonged battle, Mdina repels the invaders.

1561 The Inquisition established.

1565 The Great Siege.

1566 Founding of Valletta.

1798 Napoleon takes Malta; the Order of St John leaves the island: the Inquisition is abolished.

1799 The Maltese rise against French domination. Britain offers the islands protection.

1800 French force capitulates.

1802 Maltese Declaration of Rights asks that the islands come under the protection of the British Crown.

1814 Treaty of Paris; Malta becomes a British Crown Colony.

1914–18 World War I: Malta is known as the 'Nurse of the Mediterranean' where wounded troops go.

1921 Self-government over domestic affairs is achieved with the opening of the first Maltese Parliament.

1930 The Constitution is suspended because of Church interference.

1932 The Constitution is restored.

1933 More political unrest when the Constitution is again abolished.

1936 The Constitution is repaired: members of the Executive Council nominated.

1939–45 World War II.

1940 First Maltese citizens killed by air raids.

1942 Second Great Siege; George Cross awarded to the island for bravery.

1947 Self-government is restored.

1964 Malta becomes an independent state within the British Commonwealth.

1972 An agreement is signed with Britain and NATO allowing the use of the islands as military base.

1974 Malta becomes a Republic, but remains within the British Commonwealth.

1979 Last British forces leave.

1989 US President Bush and Soviet leader Gorbachev meet for the Malta Summit in Marsaxlokk.

1992 Queen Elizabeth II visits the islands and dedicates the World War II Siege Bell Memorial.

1996 Malta withdraws application to join European Union.

1998 Nationalists regain power, led by Dr Eddie Fenech Adami. They re-open application for EU membership.

ST. PAUL'S
ISLANDS

Qawra
Tower

Salina Bay

'aul's
ay

Bugibba

Quawra

Gallis
Tower

St. Mark's
Tower

Bur Marrad

Mosta
Fort

San Pawl
Tat-Targa

Gharghur

St. Julian's Bay

St. Julian's

Sliema
Point Tower

Mosta

Naxxar

San
Gwann

Gzira

Sliema

Cumbo
Tower

Balzan

Birkirkara

Msida

Marsamxett Harbour
Grand Harbour

Valletta

Fort St. Rocco

San Anton
Palace

Attard

Pieta

Fort St. Angelo

Kalkara

Inquisitor's Palace

Mdina

Roman Villa
Museum

MALTA

Hamrun

Floriana

Senglea

Vittoriosa

at

Hal Muxi

Qormi

Marsa

Kordin
Temples

Cospicua

Zebbug

Hal Mula

Raola

Zabbar

Verdala
Palace

Siggiewi

Hypogeum

Tarxien
Temples

Luqa

Santa
Lucia

Marsascala

Zejtun

St. Thomas Bay

Luqa Airport

Inquisitor's
Palace

Mqabba

Kirkop

Gudja

Ghar Dalam
Cave

Qrendi

Zurrieq

Safi

Marsaxlokk

Fort
St. Lucian

Hagar Qim and
Mnajdra Temples

Blue
Grotto

Nigred

Bubagra

Birzebbuga

Marsaxlokk
Bay

Fort Delimara

Wardija Tower

Kalafrana

Dolmen

Ghar Hasan
Cave

Fort Benghisa

Day 1: The Knights' City

Spend this first day exploring Valletta; explore Republic Street in the morning, then circle the city's bastions in the afternoon. A light lunch at Caffé Cordina on Republic Square, or dine more elegantly at Giannini's on St Michael's Bastion (booking essential).

—Bus terminal between Triton Fountain and City Gate; small public car park is in Floriana, facing the Hotel Phoenicia. Each half of this day takes about three hours; start with Republic Street—

Despite ugly electrical wires and TV aerials, Valletta is still a work of art. The ubiquitous enclosed wooden balconies are characteristic

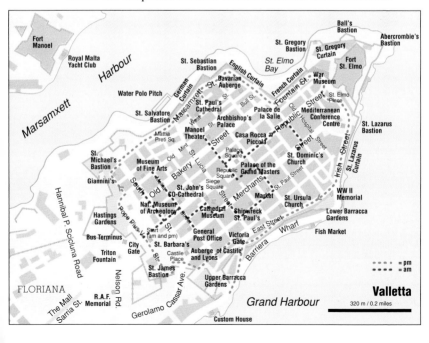

Valletta, showing the city walls

of the city and both blend and contrast gracefully with the golden sandstone of the buildings.

Pausing outside the **City Gate**, notice the moat below. Dug by Turkish slaves it is 55ft (17m) deep and 29ft (9m) wide, extending for 2,843ft (875m) between the two harbours. Once a protective barrier, it's now a car park for government officials.

Republic Street bisects Valletta, running approximately 1 mile (2km) to Fort St Elmo. It is a pedestrian precinct, but be wary of traffic zooming across it from the side streets. There's a **tourist office** in the arcade to the right of the entrance, and the ruins in the large square are those of the Royal Opera House, which was bombed in 1942.

At South Street, a left turn brings you to St Andrew's Scottish Church, then the **National Museum of Fine Arts**, between Old Mint and Vassalli streets. It is a joy to visit, especially for its magnificent collection of paintings of Malta throughout the last 500 years.

Back on Republic Street, **St Barbara's**, designed by Giuseppe Bonnici, is the parish church of the foreign community, with masses in English, Spanish, French and German. Originally the church of the Langue of Provence, it is oval in shape with a domed ceiling, delightfully bright and intimate. Across the street, the pale green interior of **St Francis's church** provides a soothing contrast.

A bit further down on the left, the **Auberge of Provence** now houses the **Museum of Archaeology**; exhibits include models of the prehistoric temples of Ggantija, Mnajdra,

Knight's armour

Hagar Qim and Tarxien, and among the finds is the original of the Fertility Goddess found in Tarxien. But the best part is the building itself, the only one of the Knights' original auberges which is open to the public. Begun in 1571, it was designed by Valletta's architect, Gerolamo Cassar.

On leaving the museum, go along Melita Street to Zachary, then turn left to take in the magnificence of **St John's Co-Cathedral**. The facade is plain, the buttressing hidden behind it. A bronze bust of Christ by Alessandro Algardi is in the pediment, and above it is a Maltese Cross, the symbol of the Knights of St John. The cathedral was designed by Gerolamo Cassar and consecrated on 20 February 1578: until 1798 it was the conventual church of the Order. It was given the title of Co-Cathedral in 1816 by Pope Pius VII as a means of ending the rivalry between Mdina and Valletta which started with the Knights' arrival way back in 1530.

It is hard to imagine a more startling difference between the church's exterior and its interior: outside it is austere; inside, it is artfully and richly decorated. It is rectangular in shape, with a barrelled interior and chapels on either side of the central chamber. The buttressing which Cassar hid with his exterior walls separates the main body of the church from the side altars. The interior is at its best when it's totally empty, and the full sweep of the 400-odd floor sepulchre slabs can be appreciated.

St John's Co-Cathedral

The bronze lecterns, dated 1557, came from the Knights' chapter church in Vittoriosa. The high altar, finished in 1686, is of lapis lazuli and in its centre is a bronze bas relief of the *Last Supper*. Giuseppe Mazzuoli created the large marble group, the *Baptism of Christ*, which is at the end of the chancel.

Seven of the eight original members of the Order have their own chapel dedicated to the patron saint of the Langue and containing the tombs of the Grand Masters. The missing member is England; as a result of Henry VIII's fight with Rome the English Knights were withdrawn from the Order.

The cathedral ceiling was bare until Mattia Preti was commissioned in 1661 to decorate it. The greatest treasure in the **Church Museum** (entrance through the third arch on the right) is a painting by Caravaggio, *The Beheading of St John the Baptist*.

Leaving St John's, go left on **Merchants' Street**, and browse in the market; take a right at St Lucia, and then a left on St Paul's

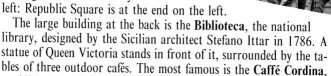

Street to reach **St Paul's Shipwreck Church**. The **Covered Market** is in the next block; a Victorian structure, the graceful building was renovated in the late 1980s. Walk through it; across the street is the back of the Palace of the Grand Masters. Pass through the arcade to your left: Republic Square is at the end on the left.

The large building at the back is the **Biblioteca**, the national library, designed by the Sicilian architect Stefano Ittar in 1786. A statue of Queen Victoria stands in front of it, surrounded by the tables of three outdoor cafés. The most famous is the **Caffé Cordina**, established in 1837 – its home-made ice-cream is wonderful.

Before continuing to Palace Square, **Great Siege Square** is a block back up Republic Street towards the city gate. The large statue is dedicated to the defenders of Malta who died during the Great Siege.

The exterior of the **Palace of the Knights** in **Palace Square** is covered with plaques commemorating historical events, including the citation King George VI wrote when he awarded the island the George Cross in 1942, and a letter from American President Franklin D Roosevelt commending the islanders for their valour. All the Grand Masters used the Palace as their headquarters until they left the island in 1798. During the British colonial period it was the Governor's headquarters, and since 1974 it has served as the Office of the President of the Republic.

Signs outside the palace may point toward the entry on the right but ignore them, and go through the **Prince of Wales entrance**

Folk dancing in Neptune's Court

In the Palace Tapestry Room

and enter **Neptune's Court**, with its subtropical plants. **Prince Alfred's Court**, named in honour of a visit by Queen Victoria's second son in 1858, is through an archway to the right. The clock dates from 1745; the hours are struck by figures representing Moorish slaves.

The public entrance to the **State Apartments** is up the small steps in a corner of the courtyard. Unfortunately tourists are not allowed to use the massive stone steps the Knights used but, once on the first floor, you can see them through the glass doors to the left.

The Knights used the **Tapestry Room** (first left) as their Council Chamber, and the Maltese parliament met here between 1921 and 1976, creating the republican government. The tapestries in the first chamber to the left were presented to the Order by Grand Master Perellos in the early 1700s. The friezes above the tapestries depict the galleys of the Order in battle against Turkish vessels.

The **Throne Room**, the Knights' Hall of St Michael and St George, contains the Great Siege frescoes, although a pair of binoculars would be handy to study them properly. Painted between 1576 and 1581, they portray the battles from the Turks' arrival at Marsaxlokk Bay in May until their withdrawal on 7 September. The small balcony on the wall opposite the throne was made from the stern of the *Grand Carrick of Rhodes*, Grand Master Adam's flagship. The **Armoury** is located on the ground floor at the back, near the Neptune courtyard. It contains one of the finest collections of weaponry in Europe, including a gold Damascene suit of armour fashioned for Grand Master Aloph de Wignacourt.

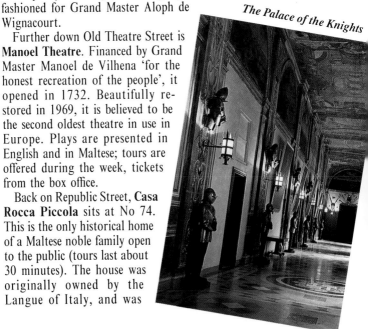

The Palace of the Knights

Further down Old Theatre Street is **Manoel Theatre**. Financed by Grand Master Manoel de Vilhena 'for the honest recreation of the people', it opened in 1732. Beautifully restored in 1969, it is believed to be the second oldest theatre in use in Europe. Plays are presented in English and in Maltese; tours are offered during the week, tickets from the box office.

Back on Republic Street, **Casa Rocca Piccola** sits at No 74. This is the only historical home of a Maltese noble family open to the public (tours last about 30 minutes). The house was originally owned by the Langue of Italy, and was

24

Casa Rocca Piccola

built soon after the Knights moved their headquarters to Valletta. It has been restored by the present marquis and contains some of the oldest examples of Maltese furniture. In the library is a set of 17th-century canvases thought to have been part of the furnishings of the Grand Master's barge of Lascaris. In the Blue Sitting Room surgical instruments used in the Knights' Hospital are displayed.

Situated between St Dominic and St Nicholas streets, the **Palace de la Salle**, a late 16th-century building, has a beautiful balcony, and was the home of Grand Master Ramon Perellos. Take a right on St Nicholas, another at Merchants, and arrive at **St Dominic's Church**. During Easter week, this is one of the places where the Last Supper is recreated.

The morning walk ends here; for lunch, adjourn to Caffé Cordina on Republic Square or, if you have booked, Giannini (see below), on the bastions, the focus of this afternoon's itinerary.

Refreshed and standing once more inside the City Gate, take a left on Ordinance Street, then another to get on to the bastions and Pope Pius V Street. A short walk to the left takes you to the top of the City Gate. To your left is **Hastings Gardens**, built on St John's Bastion and named after a former governor of the island. The gardens continue until St Michael's Bastion, offering wonderful views over Marsamxett Harbour.

Around the corner here is one of my favourite restaurants, **Giannini**. If it's sunny, try for a balcony table, but even from inside, Marsamxett Harbour, Manoel Island and Tigne Point are clearly visible. The same views are available a little lower down, from **St Andrew's Bastion**. The balconies on St Andrew's Street are some of the most attractive in the city.

The ferry to Sliema leaves from the bottom of St Mark's Street. If you are waiting for a sailing you can enjoy a drink with the locals at the **Cockney Bar**; there is also a water-polo pitch in the sea

The balcony at Giannini

here, where games are played on summer weekends.

St Paul's Anglican Cathedral has a tall steeple (the dome which looks like St Paul's Cathedral in London is actually that of the nearby Carmelite Church); take the steps beside it to explore both. St Paul's serves Malta's Anglican community; the interior is highlighted with the banner and crest of Queen Adelaide, the widow of King William IV and benefactor of the church. Built from local limestone, the interior matches the outside in simplicity. The memorial on **Piazza Indipendenza** commemorates the citizens of Valletta who were killed in the 1799 rebellion against the French; the **Auberge d'Aragon**, one of the eight buildings designed by Gerolamo Cassar for the various Langues of the Knights, is now part of the Ministry for Economic Services. Near it, on West Street, take a look at the elegant facade of **Our Lady of Pilar Church**, dating from 1670.

The **Carmelite Church** is one block up, its entrance on Old Mint Street. It replaces the one built in 1573 by Cassar, Valletta's architect, which was reduced to rubble during World War II.

Returning to Piazza Indipendenza, the steps by the red postbox take you back to the road. Continuing to the right, you're on top of the **German Curtain** and when the road makes a sharp right, **St Sebastian's Bastion** and the **Gun Post Snack Bar** are reached, the latter a good place to enjoy views of Marsamxett Harbour.

The **Bavarian Auberge**, built in 1695, is between West and St Charles streets, directly above the Jews' Sally Port, which is located in the middle of the **English Curtain**; the **French Curtain** follows,

The dome of the Carmelite Church

Barrakka Gardens

and at the end the **War Museum** is tucked into a corner of **Fort St Elmo**. The museum's prize exhibit is the George Cross. The rest details Malta's war role, including many photographs illustrating the destruction of the Three Cities (Senglea, Cospicua and Vittoriosa) and Valletta.

Crossing the end of **Republic Street**, the **Mediterranean Conference Centre** sits just around the curve of Spur Street. Originally called the Sacra Infermeria (Holy Infirmary) of the Order of the Knights of St John of Jerusalem, its construction began in 1574, and continued over the next century until it eventually reached 512ft (153m) in length. It became the world's longest hospital ward, described as 'the grandest interior in the world'.

Nursing care here was the most advanced in Europe; in a time when going into hospital could mean death from infection, the Knights' hospital pioneered hygienic procedures. The School of Anatomy and Surgery, established in 1676 by Grand Master Cottoner, was the precursor of Malta's Medical School. During World War II parts of the building were destroyed and it was not until 1978 that it was returned to glory, receiving an award for restoration work. Now used as a convention centre, it can accommodate up to 1,400 delegates. Nearby the **Malta Experience**, a 40-minute multi-media show with commentary in five languages, is shown in hourly performances, 11am–4pm.

The Greek-looking temple dominating the nearby skyline is the newest World War II memorial, dedicated by Queen Elizabeth II in 1992, 50 years after the George Cross was awarded. Up the hill the **Lower Barrakka Gardens** perch on **St Christopher's Bastion**. The small temple is a memorial to Sir Alexander Ball, a hero of the British blockade against the French between 1798 and 1799. From here, the Three Cities are across the Grand Harbour and below to the right is the old **fish market**, which dates from 1643 when it was used to quarantine arriving passengers.

You're about to arrive at my favourite street in Valletta. **St Barbara's Bastion** is not signed, but at the end of St Lucy Curtain, a little street slews off

St Barbara's Bastion

Auberge de Castille and Lyons, the Prime Minister's office

to the left. A sign indicates a dead end, but if you walk down this tree-shaded street you will come across a row of classic Maltese homes, neatly painted and shining. One of the loveliest buildings is the **Conservatorio Vincenzo Bugeja**, with elaborate balconies and delicate grille work. At night, the view from here of the illuminated bastion of the Three Cities is sheer magic.

A sharp turn left at the end of the street leads downhill through Victoria Gate. The tunnel built into the bastion at the bottom of the hill is named after Grand Master Lascaris, as are the **World War II War Rooms**. Their entrance is next to the tourist office just inside the city. Here one can see where 'Operation Husky', the July 1943 invasion of Sicily, was planned.

Retrace your steps up **Liesse Hill**. Inside Victoria Gate climb the step-streets to the entrance of the **Upper Barrakka Gardens**, which offer a magnificent view over the Grand Harbour. Looking over the edge, you will notice the Maltese word for Welcome, *Merhba*, is spelled out in shrubbery. Leaving the garden, the **Auberge de Castille and Lyons**, now the Prime Minister's office, is one of the most graceful buildings of the Maltese baroque period. The monument to Manuel Dimech (an early socialist leader) graces the centre of Castille Place and the small church next to Sir Paul Boffa's statue is **Our Lady of Victories in Valletta**, the first building erected by the Knights to thank God for deliverance from the Turks.

From Castille Place, **St James's Bastion** leads past the Central Bank of Malta, and the former **Malta Stock Exchange**. Just ahead flags fly over the City Gate, where your walk around the walls ends.

Football fan

Day 2: Rabat, Mdina and an Afternoon Cruise

A walk along the bustling streets of Rabat, Mdina's 'suburb', then through the heart of Malta's medieval 'Silent City'. Choose between three different luncheon venues, then finish with a cruise around Valletta's Grand Harbour.

—Both morning walks can be done in half a day. Take a bus to Rabat or drive to Mdina's main gate; go early to get a parking space—

Mdina, Malta's 'Silent City', is about 7 miles (11km) inland to the west of Valletta. It is one of the world's best preserved medieval cities. But before visiting the Silent City, this itinerary goes first to **Rabat**, Mdina's suburb. Head first for the **Museum of Roman Antiquities**, at the end of Museum Road beyond **Howard Gardens**. A small museum of Roman relics and statuary found nearby in 1881 has been built over the original mosaic flooring. Also known as **Roman Villa**, it leads from St Paul's Street toward the town centre.

In Parish Square, a small market operates every morning and an enormous one takes place on Sunday. Flower-sellers jostle with vegetable stall-holders and some produce is still sold direct from horse-drawn carts.

St Paul's Church, founded in 1575, stands on Parish Square and was rebuilt by Lorenzo Gafa after the 1693 earthquake. The main altar was designed by Mattia Preti and the painting above it of St Paul's shipwreck is by Stefano Erardi. The entrance to the **Grotto** is to the right of the main chapter door. Tradition holds that St Paul lived here during the three months he was on Malta and that the walls of the cave hold mystical powers of healing.

Signs point the way to Rabat's three **catacombs**, **St Cataldus**, **St Paul's**, and **St Agatha's**. They are typical of early underground Christian tombs which were also used as places of worship. St Agatha's is a fairly long walk from Parish Square, but worth it, for these are the most interesting and

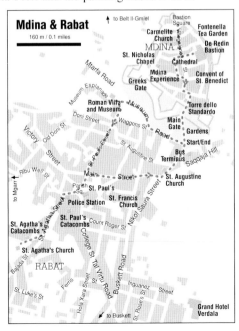

Mdina & Rabat

160 m / 0.1 miles

to Belt Il-Gmiel — Bastion Square

Fontenella Tea Garden
Carmelite Church
De Redin Bastion
MDINA
St. Nicholas Chapel
Cathedral
Mdina Experience
Convent of St. Benedict
Greeks Gate
Marfa Road
Museum Esplanade
Roman Villa and Museum
Torre dello Standardo
Doni Street
Waggons St
Main Gate
Road
Gardens
Victory Street
Old Doni St
St Augustine St
Start/End
Saqqaja Hill
Bus Terminus
Ribu Well St
Main — Street
St. Augustine Church
Parish Sq.
St. Paul's
St. Francis Church
Police Station
St. Paul's Catacombs
Count Roger St
Nikol Saura Street
St. Agatha's Catacombs
St. Agatha's Church
Bajda St
College St Tal Virtu Road
RABAT
St. Luke's St
Ferris
Hija Xara Street
Buskett Road
Inguanez Street
St. Rosa's St
Grand Hotel Verdala
to Mgarr
to Buskett

29

Market vendors in Rabat

beautiful of Rabat's catacombs. As the tunnels are very dark, it's advisable to take a map with you. The frescoes in the grotto chapel detail the life of St Agatha, who fled her native Sicily rather than marry the pagan Quintanus, Roman Governor of Catania. She returned to Catalina to be martyred in the persecutions of Emperor Decius.

Retrace your steps to Parish Square, and take the pedestrian walk though the churchyard. Note a memorial marker attesting to Paul's admiration of the Maltese people printed in eight different languages.

Turn right on Main Street and follow it to **Nikol Saura Road** where **St Augustine's** is just around the corner. Built in 1571 by Gerolamo Cassar, this church has a beautiful facade and a gilded barrel-vaulted interior. A block to the right is the first hospital built on Malta, **Santo Spirito**, which was established in the mid-1300s and served the public until 1968.

Mdina is a short walk to the left; as you approach the city gate, you'll see lines of *karozzini*, Maltese carriages, for hire. They are an enjoyable way to see Mdina, but not if you want to explore in your own time. Agree on price and duration of trip before starting out.

From every part of Malta the distinctive silhouette of Mdina looms over the landscape. At 500ft/154m, it is the highest, most defensible point on the whole of the island and the logical choice for settlement. There were Bronze Age villages here, and during the Roman era, Mdina and Rabat, then one city, was the island's capital. The Aghlabid Arabs built the defensive ditch in the late 800s, separating the city into two parts, and naming the fortified part *il-Medina* (the fortified). The Nor-

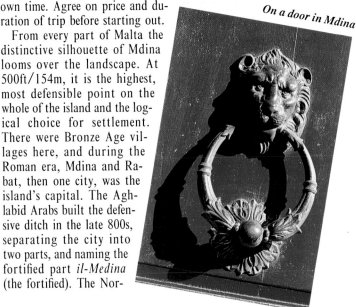

On a door in Mdina

The distinctive shape of Mdina

mans retained Mdina as their capital, the fortifications were re-strengthened, magnificent churches were built and large palazzi were constructed.

The arrival of the Knights in 1530 changed Mdina's status. They assumed the position of leadership, and power then emanated from the small town of Birgu (today's Vittoriosa).

With the building of Valletta, Mdina became known as *Citta Vecchia* (Old City). During the British reign, it held no actual power, but was home to Malta's noble families. Today it is one of the most perfect examples of a walled medieval city. The homes and churches have been maintained by their owners and the faithful, and Mdina remains a place of serene repose – thus its nickname, the Silent City.

The torches placed beside the doors of many houses are replicas of medieval street lights. The city is famed for its door-knockers and the grille-work covering the windows, behind which ladies used to sit and converse with friends outside.

A short road over a defensive moat (now filled with volleyball and tennis courts) leads through the **Main Gate** into **St Publius Square**, named in honour of Malta's first Christian who also became one of its

patron saints (St Paul and St Agatha are the others). Inside, **Torre dello Standardo** sits on the left; at one time fires were lit on the roof of the tower to warn the population when an enemy was approaching. To the right of it, the **Mdina Dungeons**, located in the Corte Capitanale, satisfies lovers of all things gory with graphic exhibits of torture and persecution. More restful, the **Museum of Natural History** (next right) is housed in the Palazzo Vilhena, an enchanting old building with a delightful courtyard. The original building on this site, destroyed by earthquake in 1693, was the seat of the *Università*, Malta's original governing body.

In the Mdina Dungeons

Villegaignon Street, named after the French knight who defended Mdina from the Turks in 1551, starts to the left and ends at Bastion Square. On the right corner is the chapel dedicated to St Agatha, built in 1417 and renovated by Lorenzo Gafa in 1694. Opposite is the Casa Inguanez, home of Malta's oldest family. To view the **Mdina Experience**, a clever blend of slides and commentary tracing Mdina's history, take **Mesquita Street** to its Piazza.

On **St Paul's Square**, two buildings beside the cathedral deserve notice: the Victorian Gothic **Casa Gourgin** and, opposite it, the **Banca Giuratale** (now the Magistrates' House), built by Vilhena for the *Università*. During the revolt against the French in 1798, it became the legislative headquarters of the resistance leaders.

But it is the **Cathedral** upon which all eyes come to rest. Its site is historic: the home of St Publius, the Maltese leader who first embraced Christianity, is reputed to have stood here. And before Roger I, the Norman Count of Sicily, built a church here around 1100, several others had stood in the same place. Roger's church

The Museum of Natural History

was destroyed by the 1693 earthquake, leaving only the apse standing. When construction of the present church was started in 1697, that apse was incorporated into the structure.

Built in the shape of a Latin cross, the interior of the Cathedral of Saint Paul is sumptuous. The memorial tablets in the nave resemble those in St John's in Valletta, showing an equal mix of the macabre and the angelic. Vincenzo and Antonio Manno created the frescoes on the ceiling; commissioned in 1794, they detail scenes from St Paul's life. In the north transept, look for Mattia Preti's painting of St Paul saving the citizens from Saracen invaders in 1422.

Tradition says that the silver processional cross accompanied Godfrey de Bouillon when he entered Jerusalem during the First Crusade. In the shrine to the left of the main altar is an icon of the Madonna, reputedly painted by St Luke, but probably Byzantine.

The **Cathedral Museum**, on the right side of Archbishop's Square across from the cathedral's entrance, contains items saved from the 1693 earthquake, 15th-century Sicilian panels which decorated the cathedral's choir, and some superb Dürer woodcuts.

The **Carmelite Church** sitting at the corner of St Peter Street is a baroque jewel with an exquisitely painted oval dome. The **Palazzo Santa Sophia**, which straddles St Sophia Street, is reputedly the oldest house in Mdina, with a cornerstone dating it back to 1388.

Bastion Square, a large open piazza, looms ahead. The view from here is terrific, and when the sky is crystal clear, Mt Etna on Sicily is visible. The dome straight ahead belongs to **Mosta's Church of the Assumption** (see *Pick & Mix Option 1*). At night, a fairyland of urban city lighting matches the sky in brilliance.

For lunch, you could either eat a

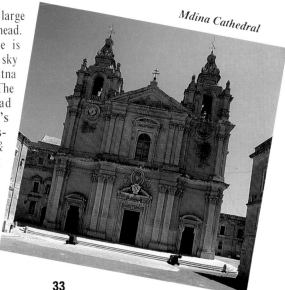

Mdina Cathedral

picnic on the bastion, go down Bastion Street to the **Fontenella Tea Garden** for a snack, or retrace your steps to Holy Cross Street for something grander at the **Medina Restaurant**.

After lunch, drive or take a taxi back across the island to the Strand in **Sliema** (opposite Valletta) where boats leave between 10am and 4pm for a cruise through Marsamxett and Grand harbours. Each cruise takes about 75 minutes and the onboard commentary is given in English, French and German.

The large yacht repair yard across Sliema Creek from the boat dock is on **Manoel Island**. Previously known as Bishop Island, it once served as a quarantine centre. The graceful, arched **Lazaretto of San Rocco**, built around 1640 and renovated in the 1720s, is one of the hospitals where incoming passengers were kept if bubonic plague was suspected. **Fort Manoel** crowns the slight hill.

The boat makes a slight dip into **Lazaretto Creek** to see the yacht basin before swinging around the peninsula of Ta'Xbiex and heading into **Marsamxett Harbour**; notice the little 'thumb' of water, called Pieta Creek. There's a Gozo cargo ferry here which departs from the Sa Maison Bastion.

As the boat cruises through Marsamxett Harbour, other Valletta

Sliema from the air

bastions rise from the water to your right. As the ship rounds the corner heading toward Fort St Elmo, the English Curtain is visible. On the promontory opposite is **Tigne Point and Fort**, the latter built in 1761 to serve, along with Fort St Elmo, as guardian of Marsamxett Harbour.

Yacht repair on Manoel Island

Next the massive bulk of **Fort St Elmo** hovers above; it's now the Malta Police Academy and home to the National War Museum. In 1565 it was the Knights' first line of defence against the Ottoman Turks in the Great Siege.

The headland on the left as you enter the **Grand Harbour** is topped by **Ricasoli Fort**. Bighi Hospital occupies the tip of the second peninsula and **Fort St Angelo** is at the head of the third, on a site occupied since Phoenician times. After Fort St Elmo fell in the Great Siege, Fort St Angelo bore the full brunt of the Ottoman attack, but the walls stood firm. Today, the fort is being restored to its former glory by the Knights of St John.

Tug boats are berthed at the head of the creek, next to the South Gate Dry Docks. The district of **Senglea** fills the last 'finger'; **St Michael's Fort**, also an important cornerstone in the Knights' defences against the Turks, was here but much of it, along with Senglea itself, was destroyed by World War II bombings. It offers fantastic views of Valletta.

The final sight on this side of the Grand Harbour is the **Malta Dry Docks**, which are easily recognised by the massive cranes rising into the air. During World War II the docks were subject to the most intense bombardment in the world: 69 consecutive days.

The tour returns

The boat turns around here, putting Valletta on your left, and makes its way back to its base at Sliema.

Option 1. A Central Circle

Explore the gardens of San Anton Palace; shop for souvenirs at the Ta'Qali Crafts Centre; see Mosta's church dome; and finish the day at St Helen's in Birkirkara.

—A car is necessary, as no direct bus service links the towns—

From Valletta, take the road to Rabat. About 1 mile (1.5km) beyond Farson's Brewery, a very small sign points right to **San Anton Gardens**. If you miss it, take the next right (almost immediately) and double back. San Anton Palace and gardens are a block off the main road.

The palace was the country residence of the Grand Masters from the early 17th century and in the British colonial era it was used as the governor's residence. Since 1974 it has been the official residence of the President of the Republic of Malta.

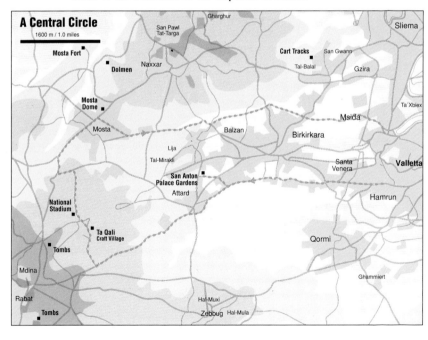

Glass-blower at Ta Qali

The gardens display an astonishing variety of sub-tropical flowers. If you walk anti-clockwise, the Eagle Fountain adorned with cherubs comes first. Looking straight ahead you'll see the main central pond and the entrance to the palace. The nearest arch leads into a small zoo, behind which is a miniature five-storey pagoda, presented by the Japan Cherry Blossom Foundation.

The inviting terrace which fronts the palace is backed by an ivy-covered wall and two stone chairs flank the entrance. The only part of the palace open to the public is the colonnade leading to a back entrance of the gardens. The green doors on the right of it lead to the president's office.

Leaving San Anton Gardens return to the main road and take a right toward Rabat. Be prepared for the right turn to **Ta'Qali** as soon as the lighting towers of the National Stadium come into view on the right. The **Crafts Village** is located on the World War II airfield. Pottery, lace-making, weaving, silver-working and glass-blowing are a few of the traditional Maltese crafts demonstrated here. Mdina Glass is the best known and largest business of its kind and it is fascinating to watch the craftsmen at work.

Exit the way you entered, but follow the signs to **Mosta**. When you come to the T-junction, go left towards Rabat. At the next T, where the main road is joined, take a right, and the dome of Mosta will be just ahead. This is a less travelled road, bringing you into Mosta on a more picturesque route. Follow the street into the centre of town; at the church square take a left and then a right to the church parking space.

Mosta's dome is a landmark throughout the island; 122ft (37m) in diameter, it is the fourth largest unsupported dome in Europe, smaller only than the Pantheon, St Peter's in Rome and the Basilica Xewkija, Gozo. The ceiling is decorated with a geometric diamond pattern.

Celebrations over Mosta

Feast Day, St Helen's

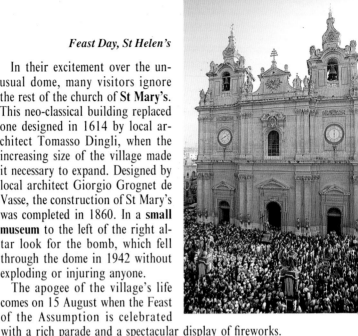

In their excitement over the unusual dome, many visitors ignore the rest of the church of **St Mary's**. This neo-classical building replaced one designed in 1614 by local architect Tomasso Dingli, when the increasing size of the village made it necessary to expand. Designed by local architect Giorgio Grognet de Vasse, the construction of St Mary's was completed in 1860. In a **small museum** to the left of the right altar look for the bomb, which fell through the dome in 1942 without exploding or injuring anyone.

The apogee of the village's life comes on 15 August when the Feast of the Assumption is celebrated with a rich parade and a spectacular display of fireworks.

To reach **Birkirkara** (B'Kara on signs), one of Malta's most historic parishes, take the road to Valletta. Ignore the 'B'Kara Centre' sign and go left on the by-pass road (signed St Julian's). At the second roundabout, take the right (third) exit – no signs, but the dome and belfries of **St Helen's** are clearly visible – and park here.

In 1436, when Malta was deemed too large for only two parishes (Mdina and Birgu – now Vittoriosa), 10 more were created, Birkirkara among them. In 1630, Pope Urban VIII issued a Papal Bull making it the first parish collegiate on Malta. A more singular papal honour bestowed by Pius X in 1912 is seen during the parade to mark the Feast Day of St Helen (the Sunday following 18 August) when a liveried man carrying a silver mace precedes the canons.

Mace carrier, St Helen's

The present church stands on the site of an earlier one which was destroyed in the 1693 earthquake. St Helen's was designed by a local architect, Domenico Cachia, and since its completion in 1745 has been considered one of the finest examples of Maltese ecclesiastical architecture.

Designed in a classic baroque Latin cross, the interior is 180ft (55m) long and 117ft (36m) wide with a large dome centred over the main altar. The frescoes are relatively new, completed between 1906 and 1910, depicting scenes in the life of St Helen.

To avoid getting tangled up in Birkirkara's one-way streets, it's best to head home the way you came.

Explore the cities of Senglea, Cospicua and Vittoriosa.

–Takes four to five hours. Start near Senglea and finish at Bighi Hospital. Plenty of opportunities for cold drinks. Buses back to base–

The Three Cities were originally called il-Birgu, l-Isla and Bormla, but after the Great Siege were renamed Vittoriosa, Senglea and Cospicua. The fortifications which surround Cospicua are the result of several centuries of building in the wake of the siege. The Margherita Lines which ran from French Creek to Kalkara Creek were designed by Marculano da Firenzuloa in 1638; the Cotonera Lines outside them were built between 1670 and 1680, forming a semi-circular shape with a circumference of 3 miles (5km). The two rings formed a secure line of defence in which over 40,000 people could be housed in times of war. Today, most of the bastions are surrounded by apartment buildings and have had tunnels dug through them for traffic access.

From Sliema and Valletta drivers should follow signs to the airport and Three Cities; at the Three Cities roundabout take the Paola exit (the first one), stay on this road until the second roundabout, then take the Cospicua exit, drive through St Helen's Gate in the Margherita Bastions, and park on St Paul Square. To get into **Senglea**, walk along Triq Il-Mons. Alternatively, take a bus to Senglea and ask the driver to let you off before **St Michael's Gate**.

Claude de la Sengle, after whom the city is now named, fortified the walls in 1554 and built Fort St Michael. After Fort St Elmo fell during the Great Siege, Fort St Michael (dismantled in 1922), and Fort St Angelo became the primary target of the Ottoman

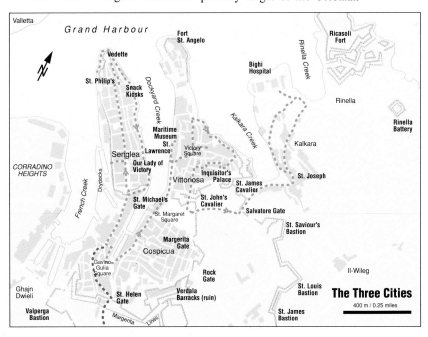

The Vedette with Valletta in the distance

guns, and a great chain was stretched across the points of the 'fingers' with a bridge of boats that allowed the defenders to move men easily between the two. The peninsula suffered bombardment again during World War II because of the nearby dry docks.

Inside the gates, on the left, is **Our Lady of Victory Church**. The modern monument is dedicated to the residents of the Three Cities killed between 1940 and 1943. Just beyond it, take a left up the steps of **Triq San Pietru U San Pawl** and peer over the wall at the end for a direct look into the heart of the docks.

Return to the main street; on **Pjazza L-Erbgha Ta'Settembru** is a copy of the Madonna and Child statue which used to stand in front of Our Lady of Victory Church, often called the 'Miracle Madonna' because it remained unscathed by bombs. Stop for a moment and look at the pleasing pattern the balconies make as they lead the eye up Triq il-Vittorja toward the baroque **St Philip's Church** on Pjazza Francesco Zahra Pittur.

To the right of the church then left on Triq Iz-Zewg Mini will quickly bring you to the **Safe Haven Garden** and some wonderful views over the harbour to Valletta. Here stands the **Vedette**, an old look-out point famous for the eyes and ears sculpted on it. (The pelican is a symbol for Christian love.) At the park's entrance, go down the steps to the left for a walk around the point.

Throughout this walk, you'll run across many clubs where members work on their *dghajsas* – that distinctive boat reminiscent of a Venetian gondola but highly decorated in bright colours; there are annual boat races. Once these boats worked as ferries, transporting people between the towns surrounding the Grand Harbour.

Retrace your steps around the 'tip'. Towards the head of the bay, stepped streets lead

'Fingers' of the Three Cities

Senglea balconies

steeply up; both the **Alice Springs** and **Prince Charles** kiosks are good for a snack or a cold drink.

The archway ahead signals the end of Senglea. The dry docks prevent walking by the water's edge so you will need to walk back to San Pawl Square and continue downhill to Gavino Gulia Square where the bus terminal (if you're ready to call it a day) and the Malta South Gate Dry Docks are located.

Cospicua was Malta's worst casualty in World War II: over 90 percent of the town was flattened. Unfortunately, rebuilding here has not been undertaken with much care. Around the curve of the bay, several flights of steps lead to the **Church of the Immaculate Conception**. Nearby is **Maxim's**, selling a variety of the local speciality: cheesecake. Down the hill and back on the main road, cross to the left (water) side and follow the walls. Here the Bormla Boat and Regatta Club welcomes visitors.

At the crest of the hill is **Vittoriosa**, known in medieval times as Birgu. It was the first Sicilian-Norman capital. When the Knights arrived in 1530, they made Birgu their base. After the Great Siege,

In the harbour at Vittoriosa

the city was re-named Vittoriosa, but when the Knights moved to their new capital, Valletta, the power structure went with them.

At the end of the street into Vittoriosa, palm trees surround the four statues of the monument which commemorates the closing of the last British base in 1979. Before exploring the church of **St Lawrence** which is behind it, visit the **Maritime Museum**, in a former Royal Navy bakery.

Leaving the Maritime Museum, walk towards **Fort St Angelo**, which, after a period of distintegration, is being restored to its past glory – and for possible future use as a museum. From here there are wonderful views over the Grand Harbour.

Back in the square fronting the church, St Lawrence was the first conventual church of the Order and contains many relics of the Knights. Built in 1691, the church shares with the **Oratorio of St Joseph** (located at the rear) the site of Santo Maria Damascene where the Knights worshipped when they arrived on the island from Rhodes in 1530.

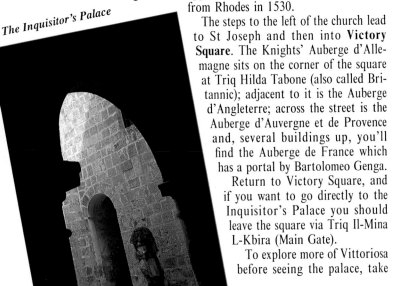

The Inquisitor's Palace

The steps to the left of the church lead to St Joseph and then into **Victory Square**. The Knights' Auberge d'Allemagne sits on the corner of the square at Triq Hilda Tabone (also called Britannic); adjacent to it is the Auberge d'Angleterre; across the street is the Auberge d'Auvergne et de Provence and, several buildings up, you'll find the Auberge de France which has a portal by Bartolomeo Genga.

Return to Victory Square, and if you want to go directly to the Inquisitor's Palace you should leave the square via Triq Il-Mina L-Kbira (Main Gate).

To explore more of Vittoriosa before seeing the palace, take

Bocci players

Triq San Filippu at the north-west corner of the square, then at the end of it go down the steps by the red post-box. At the bottom is a *bocci* field; bowls is played throughout the Mediter-ranean, but on Malta, in-stead of using wooden or metal balls, bowlers use solid cylindrical pieces of wood. The bar un-derneath the *bocci* field serves cold drinks. Once refreshed, follow the wall uphill.

At **Triq il-Manolragg** the best views end; at the square, take the road going right and follow it to Triq Il-Kwartier which leads into Triq Pacifiku Scicluna; at the end go left on to Triq Papa Alessan-dru. At its end, take a right on to Triq Il-Palazz Ta'L-Isqof and the entrance to the **Inquisitor's Palace** is on the right.

The Inquisition or Holy Office was established in Malta in 1562, with the role of protecting the Catholic faith by any means. Of the 62 Inquisitors in Malta, two became Popes, and 22 gained the red cardinal's hat. The Inquisitors left when the French captured the island in 1798 and in the 19th century the building was used as officers' quarters.

The present building was constructed in the 1530s and although the interior has not been properly furnished the timbered ceil-ings are among the best on the island. Be-neath the public rooms are the dungeons.

Leave Vittoriosa via the **Gate of Provence**, and you can either return to your car (or wait for a bus at the nearby stop), or turn left and continue down the hill. If you go for the latter you are officially leaving the Three Cities, but tiny **Kalkara** is worth seeing. The large church which sits at the head of Kalkara Creek is the beauti-

Traditional boat design

fully austere **St Joseph**. The main sanctuary is of native sandstone and the altar is bare except for a set of candlesticks and a statue of Christ on the Cross. Climb the hill to-wards the graceful 19th-century neo-classical **Bighi Hospital**, where the troops of Napoleon and Nelson were treated. During World War I the hospital was known as the 'nurse of the Mediterranean'. During the Great Siege a Turkish battery operated from **Fort Ricasoli**, on the seaward point across Rinella Creek, but it is now falling into disrepair.

Visit the prehistoric ruins of Borg in-Nadur and Ghar Dalam, the port of Birzebbuga, and the fishing villages of Marsaxlokk and Marsascala. Take swimming gear and a picnic lunch for Peter's Pool; book ahead to dine at Gabriel in Marsascala (tel: 684194).

—A full day for a walker (about 10 miles/16km), or a driver who wants to swim at Peter's Pool or hike around Delimara peninsula—

Approaching **Birzebbuga** from Valletta, look out for the small sign on the left indicating **Ghar Dalam** (Cave of Darkness). If you miss it, make a U-turn at the bottom of the hill. (The bus stops opposite the entrance.) The museum here holds fossilised deer, bears, dwarf elephants and hippopotami dating back to the Neolithic and Pleistocene eras, but the best relics are in the Museum of Archaeology in Valletta. Similar fossils have been discovered on Sicily fuelling the theory that the islands were once connected, forming a land bridge between Europe and Africa.

The prehistoric site of **Borg in-Nadur** is also easy to miss; park close to the bus stop at the bottom of the hill, then follow the rocky track to the ruins. The complex dates from 1400BC and includes the remains of a megalithic temple, a few beehive-shaped stone houses, and a defensive wall.

South East Malta

The charm of Birzebbuga itself is almost lost in the overwhelming presence of the nearby ship container terminal. You can stop at the marker near Kalafrana which commemorates the visit of Gorbachev and Bush in December 1989 for their summit meeting. Just beyond it is Pretty Bay, a white sandy beach ringed with attractively-painted homes.

Retrace your steps but now keep to the coast road. Cresting the hill, **Marsaxlokk**, (pronounced *Marsa-shlock*) a picturesque fishing village, is ahead on the left. Marsaxlokk is renowned for its Sunday market (which also operates during the week, but only for tourist goods). Walking around the bay you will see fish and boats being cleaned and nets being untangled, folded and put away.

Deep waters at Peter's Pool

Drivers should leave Marsaxlokk via the Valletta road. Walkers should follow the bay, staying well above the power station. Just after the church take a right on Triq San Giuseppe, then another on Triq Melquart. At the roundabout at the top of the hill take the first exit and stay to the left; **Delimara** is a right turn about 100 yards (100m) beyond. At the first fork in the track take a right for Point Delimara (left goes to the lighthouse). Driving along the crest, you're rewarded with wonderful views of Marsaxlokk and Birzebbuga. Note a sign pointing the way to the car park for **Peter's Pool**.

The road ends at Fort Delimara, not much further on. For an almost private swimming pool all to yourself, walk down to **Slug's Pool** or **Long Bay** to swim; otherwise head for the more popular Peter's Pool. Be careful driving down the track as it is extremely rough. One word of caution: thieves operate in this region, and will casually break your car windows. The best defence is to leave the windows open and nothing valuable inside.

The path down to the pool is a well-trodden one; there's no shore, and you can dive into the very deep, clear, blue water from the rocky shelving. Beware the currents which swirl under the rocky outcrops at the pool's end. You can also explore the peninsula; paths are obvious and it's hard to get lost.

After a picnic and a swim, return to the main road and follow the signs to **St Thomas**

Marsaxlokk harbour

Bay. At the next big junction (Zejtun is to the left), go right and you will begin a meandering run through uninhabited countryside. If you are on foot, take the more direct path along the shore as far as St Thomas Bay. Along with craggy cliffs, look for salt pans, hidden bays, a communications satellite, the ruins of St Paul's Church, and carpets of wild flowers. At St Thomas Bay continue around the water or go directly to Marsascala. At the next major intersection, the road turns right and follows the bay and passes St Thomas Bar and Restaurant and the Southern Surfing Club. The latter is private, but a sail board or boat can be hired.

The one-way system makes getting out of St Thomas complicated, but eventually signs will direct you into the village of **Marsascala**, a resort popular with the locals. Unlike many of the fishing villages along the coast, Marsascala has managed to retain its character. Entering the village can be confusing.

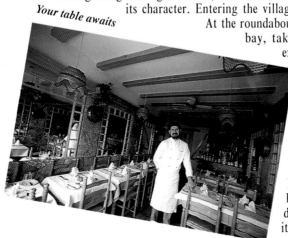

Your table awaits

At the roundabout at the head of the bay, take the right (third) exit; follow the road towards Zonqor Point until signs direct you into the town centre.

A good choice for dinner is **Gabriel**, a seafood restaurant on the Bay. It's expensive but has acquired a devoted following for its excellent seafood.

Option 4. Quarries and Temples

Explore one of Malta's stone-working quarries; take a boat ride through the Blue Grotto; visit the prehistoric temples of Hagar Qim and Mnajdra.

–A 2-hour morning or afternoon excursion. If you make it morning, why not take a picnic? A car is essential–

The quarries which supply Malta's building stone are near **Mqabba**; follow signs to the airport, south of Valletta. Approaching a roundabout where the airport is within sight, take the third (right) marked **Kirkop**. You'll pass under a runway; at the next two roundabouts, take the third (right) exit at each, signed – among others – Mqabba.

From here the road is lined with quarries surrounded by fences; find one that is being worked and look down. Many are up to 60ft (18m) deep, with a maximum working depth of around 80ft (24m).

Leaving Mqabba, follow the signs for Hagar Qim; at the first roundabout, go straight on (direction Hagar Qim and Qrendi); 100ft (30m) later, look for a left turn (unsigned but it leads to **Zurrieq**). Within a few minutes a fantasy castle, pagodas and cacti made from coloured pebbles appear on the central reservation.

Once you've seen the artwork, take a right. The **Blue Grotto** is under 5 minutes away. Consisting of several caves and grottos, it gets its name from reflections in the water of the colourful corals and minerals embedded in the limestone. From the parking lot, follow signs to the landing stage. The Grotto cruise lasts about 30 minutes and is subject to weather conditions.

Quarrying stone

After the cruise, take a left turn several hundred yards up the road and **Hagar Qim** is less than a mile (2km) away. This prehistoric temple overlooking the sea is made of globigerina limestone. The name means 'standing stones' and some of the slabs are among the largest in the world. A temple of the Ggantija period, Hajar Qim has unusual carvings which do not appear anywhere else in Malta.

Down the hill the sister temple, **Mnajdra**, is beautifully sited over-

Visiting the Blue Grotto

looking the sea. (Opposite it is **Filfla** island; once used by the British for target practice, it's now a nature reserve.) Dating from 3000BC to 1500BC, Mnajdra was built from coralline limestone and consists of three temples, with a common outside wall.

Seen from above, the chambers of the middle temple resemble a woman's body. People believed that a Goddess of Fertility controlled the elements which ensured a fruitful harvest. The temples were used for sacrificial purposes, and gifts of milk and blood were presented at the altars. Note the square holes in the Oracle chamber, where priests spoke to worshippers without being seen.

Enjoy your picnic here or, if it's early evening, watch the sunset.

5. The South Coast

From Rabat, visit Verdala Palace, Buskett Gardens; the prehistoric cart tracks and caves at 'Clapham Junction', and walk along Dingli Cliffs.

—Easily walked in a day (about 7 miles/11km). Less than 2 hours by car (add walking time on cliffs). An infrequent bus service exists. Take a picnic—

Leaving Rabat, the road to Verdala passes St Dominic's Church; **Verdala Palace** is less than 1½ miles (2km) on the left. Built by Grand Master Hugues Louvenx de Verdale in 1586 as his summer residence, and later serving as a British governors' summer residence, it sits in a commanding position, surrounded by gardens, with views all over Malta. Designed by Gerolamo Cassar, it has rare corner cupboards of Gozo marble and a graceful, oval staircase. The small **chapel** in the grounds is late 16th century, dedicated to St Anthony the Abbot.

Exiting the palace, **Buskett Gardens** (from the Italian *boschetto* for 'small wood'), Malta's only true forest, is a short downhill walk. In December and January when oranges are harvested, their aroma permeates the air. The snack bar offers cold drinks and light refreshments and the gardens are a popular picnic spot. They are also the site of great activity on the eve of 29

Clapham Junction cart tracks

June, when *Mnajra*, the feast of Saints Peter and Paul, is celebrated.

Near Buskett, a sign points to **Clapham Junction**, site of the prehistoric cart tracks and caves which were inhabited until the 19th century. At the end of a road which looks like a car park, turn left; near the top of the small hill, the cart tracks are indicated left; park at the end.

Some historians think the grooves were man-made so people would follow a specific route; others that the stones eroded with continual use. The **caves**, about 300ft (92m) along the upper path, are the only ones in the area.

Returning to your car, go back down the hill and cross the top of the 'car park'. At the first T-junction head left; the road rolls through countryside, eventually passing the **Inquisitor's Palace**, on the left behind an elaborate gate. Visitors are not allowed access, but the guards will let you walk around the outside.

A few minutes later the road rounds a bend and the sea can be seen several hundred yards below. From here the road leads to **Dingli**, about 2 miles (3km) away, and there are stunning views of the south coast. The cliffs fall sharply to the sea, and it is an ideal place for walking. If you came by bus, wait for your return trip at the **Giardino del Paradiso** restaurant.

Above the steep cliffs at Dingli

Option 6. Exploring Malta's Tail

A morning or afternoon drive through a sparsely populated area; visits include the Shrine of Saint Mary of Mellieha, the Red Tower, and Popeye's Village. Take a picnic or return to the Arches Restaurant in Mellieha for lunch.

–Start at Pwales Beach, at the head of St Paul's Bay.
A car is essential for this tour–

Round the bend near the top of the first hill as you drive up from the bay is the **Selmun Palace**, an 18th-century building designed by Domenico Cachia. Continue on to the roundabout, take the exit marked **Mellieha Centre** and continue through the town, noting the location of the Arches Restaurant on the left about 100ft (30m) before the entrance to Our Lady Chapel.

Instead of parking by the entrance, continue for about 40ft (12m) and take the first left around the base of **Mellieha Church**. At the top is a cemetery and a children's playground, and you can park nearby. After sightseeing, the nearby **Sea View Café** is a wonderful place for a cold drink on a hot morning. From the terrace of the small bar, Mellieha Bay is spread out below with the White Tower on Marfa Ridge clearly visible.

Walk back to see **Our Lady Chapel**, one of the oldest and most venerated on the island. It is small and hewn from a rock; legend says that St Paul may have prayed in this grotto after he was shipwrecked off Malta's coast. Particularly lovely are the 11th-century frescoes which surround the upper walls and chapel roof.

To get on to the 'tail', leave the Sea View and return to the main road; head left and downhill, past the crescent-shaped, sandy

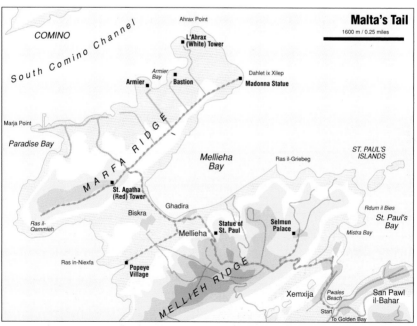

Golden Bay

Il-Ghadira Beach, one of Malta's largest and most popular. The road behind it is perpetually crowded in high summer.

Climbing the hill, the fortress at the top is the **Red Tower** (currently being renovated); take a left at the roundabout at the top of the ridge opposite the 'Armier, Little Armier' road. There are great views from here, but unfortunately they are marred by electric power lines. If you want to explore on foot, take the semi-dirt road past the tower to **Ras il-Qammieh** at the south of the tail.

To reach its north end, return to the main road and take the road opposite which runs along the top of **Marfa Ridge** with Mellieha Bay below on the right. This is an area where many Maltese come in the summer, and from the cliffs you'll see many anchored boats, the occupants picnicking on them or swimming off the nearby rocks. Several roads lead the other way off this main route (none interconnect, so you must retrace your steps to the main road) including the one to Armier (second one), which hosts regular celebrations after every major *festa*. At **Dahlet ix Xilep** there's a small statue of the Madonna and a Lady Chapel near the point, and from here, the **White Tower** is a 15–20 minute walk away.

Return to the main road, and Il-Ghadira, following signs to **Popeye Village** which was built for the 1981 movie starring Robin Williams. To end the excursion, return the way you came. There are good spots for picnics around here, or you could head straight to Mellieha for lunch at the Arches.

To enjoy a variety of water sports, **Golden Bay** (well signed) is only a 5-minute drive away.

Option 7. A Night on the Town

Dine at a table overlooking St Julian's Bay; wander over to the Casino for a spot of gambling before dancing the night away at a nearby nightclub.

Malta has never been known for wild nightlife, but as tourism has increased, so has the number of night-time establishments. Most are located in the St Julian's/Paceville area by Sliema. Traffic, especially on the weekends, is impossible, and you'll spend more time looking for a parking place than dining or dancing. So leave the car behind, and walk or use taxis.

In the Casino

My favourite restaurant, the **San Giuliano**, overlooks Spinola Bay. (If it's full, try the nearby **La Dolce Vita**, or the **Baracuda**.) Dress is smartly casual; jackets are not required, but they will be at the Casino later. There are some wonderful pasta dishes – Fettuccini Alfredo is a classic; and if fresh fish is on the menu, try it lightly grilled, sprinkled with lemon juice and olive oil.

After an espresso or two, a short walk on Church Street leads to Dragonara Road with the **Casino** at the end of the drive. In the richly-decorated main room, you can play slot machines, roulette and blackjack; for those wishing to wager larger sums of money, there is *chemin de fer*.

The Casino will stay open as long as people wish to play, but if you want to spend your winnings (or forget your losses) go clubbing: **Euphoria** and **Axis** in Paceville are within walking distance.

The exteriors of the discos are unremarkable, but inside, the laser beam never stops, nor does the music. Getting a drink can be difficult, but the cover charges ensure that management doesn't lose out. Both places are busy from about 10pm onwards, but neither gets into top gear until after midnight, by which time most of the island has shut down (see also Nightlife section on page 86 for further information).

The San Giuliano restaurant; dancing in Euphoria (right).

According to legend, Gozo is Calypso's Isle, an enchanted place where the nymph kept Odysseus happily in bondage for seven years. Standing upon one of the many terraced hills you can see why he didn't try to escape; many modern visitors never wish to leave either.

The history of Gozo has paralleled that of its larger neighbour, but during the Phoenician and Roman periods Gozo was treated as a country apart from Malta and given its own names, *Gwl* followed later by *Gaulus*. When the Saracen Arabs ruled both islands, Gozo remained predominantly Christian. Under the Sicilians, it was granted a separate *Università*; the period of Spanish rule left a new name, Gozo (Spanish for 'joy'). The Arabic name (pronounced *ow-desh*) returned in the 1500s, and this is in fact the way Gozitans refer to their island today.

The Knights treated Malta and Gozo equally. Less protected than Malta, Gozo suffered more from pirate attacks, the worst of these in 1551 when the Ottoman Turks ransacked the island. Gozo had a short period of independence between 1798 and 1800 when the Maltese were ruled by the French. Under the British, Malta and Gozo were united. Gozo has its own bishop and cathedral, and has been an independent diocese since 1864.

Fishing boat's decorative eye

Nine miles (14km) in length and 4 miles (6km) at its widest point, Gozo has a shoreline 85 miles (137km) long, and is one third the size of Malta, but it never feels crowded except near Marsalforn and Xlendi in July and August. The ferry crossing from Malta is short at only 25 minutes, but the difference between the two islands is marked: the northwestern end of Malta is rocky and barren, whereas Gozo's ferry harbour is surrounded by lush vegetation. Behind the harbour, gently terraced fields climb the flat-topped hills, many crowned with villages which were built for defensive purposes.

Fishing and farming are primary sources of income on Gozo although tourism is a close third. Because the fields are small and built on terraces, most work still has to be done without the aid of tractors, so donkey carts are common.

Day 1: The Island's Historical Core

Walk through the capital, Victoria, and its Citadel; lunch on local specialities at Gesthers, in Xaghra; then visit Ggantija prehistoric temple before ending the day at Gozo Heritage.

—A day trip from Malta. Victoria and the Citadel take half a day. Public transport is feasible but confirm bus departure times and note that you must change buses when travelling from Xaghra to Gozo Heritage—

St George

There is parking in Victoria behind the bus depot but come early, as most spaces are gone by 9.30am. You could have breakfast at **Frankie's Garden Tavern**: the service is good and the food homemade. The CNS bookshop across the road and the Book Rose on Republic Street both sell foreign language newspapers. The **Tourist Office** is at the corner of Palm Street; then comes the Post Office (open all day); across the street is the Astra Theatre.

At **Pjazza Indipendenza** (known locally as **It Tokk**) is a World War II memorial. The other monumental building is the **Banca Giuratale**, erected in 1733 by Grand Master Vilhena. The **Central Café** here serves a great cappuccino.

To enter the labyrinth which forms Victoria's oldest part (**Il Borgo**), take the short street by **Gangu's Bar** (a favourite with the locals, as is the nearby **Ginevra**). During the week it's a mini-market, selling a variety of fresh vegetables. **St George's Square** is at the end, and the eye is drawn to the magnificent facade of the baroque church of the same name. Built in 1678, it is, quite simply,

The Citadel in Victoria, Gozo's capital

St George's, showing altar canopy and frescoes

stunning. Constructed in the shape of a cross, it is a seamless mixture of the old and the new. The altar, installed in 1967, is a copy of one which Bernini carved for St Peter's in Rome, and the dome and ceiling paintings are also modern.

The canopy over the altar has a gilded angel at each corner; there is a painting by Mattia Preti, and ornate carved pillars surround the side altars. Despite the baroque richness, there is a feeling of warmth and serenity.

To the right of the church, St George Street leads along a winding, meandering route with small shops and old houses. Note the balconies and the doors painted in a shade known as Gozo green.

At the first T-junction, take a right and then an almost immediate left. At a junction with a large statue of St George on the corner building, go left, and the street shortly opens on to **Piazza**

Santu Wistin. The south side of the square is terraced with beautiful, two-storey Gozitan-style homes, each with a typical enclosed balcony above the centre door. At the far end is the 19th-century **Church of St Augustine**, which is flanked by four statues.

Return the way you came and take a right on **Triq Il-Karita**, then a left at the first T-junction up School Street. Next comes my favourite part of Victoria. Look for a statue of the Madonna and a Child accepting bread rolls from a kneeling supplicant, then go right. This is **Narrow Street**, a long courtyard where women work on their lace patterns and children play. Ignore the electric wires running overhead, and you could be in another century.

Return to the street from which you came, and go right. The road opposite St James's Church leads straight up to the **Citadel**; climb to the tree-shaded terrace opposite for a view of the massive fortifications and the cathedral.

In the citadel's **Piazza Katidral** are three main buildings: the cathedral takes centre stage; on its left the Law Courts are in the 17th-century **Palace of the Governors**, the right is filled with the **Chapter Hall**, built in 1899, and the **Bishop's Palace** which before 1551 was a residence of the Hakem of Gozo.

The Church of the Assumption, better known as the **Cathedral**, was designed by Lorenzo Gafa and built between 1697 and 1711 on the site of an earlier temple dedicated to Juno. It is best known for its *trompe*

In Piazza Santu Wistin

l'oeil dome. Painted by Antonio Manuele Poggo in 1739, it only gives the appearance of being a dome; the ceiling is actually flat.

Before taking a walk around the bastions, spend some time in the citadel's five small museums. The **Folklore Museum** is off Triq Il-Fosse in three 16th-century houses which are as interesting as the excellent exhibits. The **Cathedral Museum**, further up Il-Fosse, has some of the columns from the Juno temple. Back in the square, the **Armoury** and **Natural Science Museums** are opposite each other on Quarters Street, beyond the house with the shrine to Ta'Pinu on it. The **Archaeology Museum** is located through the small arch to the right of the cathedral square in the Palazzo Bondi and contains relics from prehistoric Gozo through Punic, Roman, Byzantine and Arabic eras, to medieval tombstones.

Next make a stop at the **Crafts Centre** and **Lace Workshop** located in former cells on Prison Street, then climb the wide steps to **St Michael's Bastion**. Walk in a clockwise direction; a set of steps leads to a walkway across the top of the citadel's entrance, with the best views of the Piazza. On **St Martin's Bastion** a bar serves local wines, beers, and soft drinks. It's one of the few places open in Victoria on Sunday afternoon.

To continue along the bastions, climb the steps to **St Martin's Cavalier**; to the right are the ruins of buildings which were destroyed in the great earthquake of 1692. The walkway starts to curve and the wall here is too high to see over. At the telescope, however, the view returns: look for the Cross of St Joseph with glimpses of Marsalforn, the

Windmill at Xaghra

The north coast beyond Xaghra

fishing village and popular beach resort, in the distance behind it.

Take the long flight of steps down to the rear of the citadel. Here the invincibility of the walls and their massive thickness can be fully appreciated. You can make a circuit through the lower part, walking the narrow streets edged by high walls and ruins. To reach the bus terminus or car park again, return to Republic Street and retrace your steps. From here it's a 5-minute drive or 15 minutes on the bus to **Xaghra** (only one bus plies the route). **Gesther's**, only open at noon, is a small restaurant and has good local specialities. It's on the main street coming from Victoria near the town square. Or in the square try **Oleander**, one of the island's most fashionable, but casual, restaurants. Park your car at Ggantija and walk the remaining 500ft (154m) or so, stopping by the windmill, one of the few on the island with its vanes intact.

It is difficult to date the temple of **Ggantija** (which means 'female giant'); the best estimates are between 3600BC to 3000BC, but it is among the oldest free-standing stone buildings ever discovered. There are actually two separate temples, each with its own entrance but sharing a circular forecourt. Some parts of the perimeter walls rise to 20ft (6m), containing megalithic stones weighing up to 50 tons (45,000kg). According to myth, it was a female giant, Sansuna, who brought the stones here on her head from Ta'Cenc.

To reach Gozo Heritage by bus, ask the driver to let you off at the Mgarr/Victoria road; there should be less than a 20-minute wait for another bus heading to Mgarr/Ferry. If you're driving, follow the signs to Mgarr/Malta Ferry; **Gozo Heritage** is on the left just beyond St Cecilia's Tower. Located in a renovated farmhouse, the exhibits cover the 6,000 years of Gozitan history from the Stone Age to independence.

From here, it's a 5-minute drive back to the ferry to Malta.

Option 1. A Ring around the Island

Circle Gozo, starting where the ferry arrives; visit Nadur, Dahlet Qorrot, Ramla Bay, Calypso's Cave, Marsalforn, the Salt Pans, Zebbug, Gharb, the shrine of Ta'Pinu, Fungus Rock, the Azure Window, Xlendi, Mgarr Ix-Xini, and the domed church of Xewkija.

—Allow a full day. You need a car. The itinerary is planned to avoid Victoria, but head for it if you lose your way—

Leaving the ferry harbour, take the road to **Nadur**. Driving towards the town, the windmills to your right are in Qala, among the last of many which once dotted the countryside.

The church of **Saints Peter and Paul**, built in 1760, dominates Nadur's main square. Drive north from the church square and at Triq Dicembru 13 take a left, another at the T-junction, and at the next one a right. There should be signs to

Ramla Bay

San Blas Bay and **Dahlet Qorrot**. At the first fork, go left to San Blas Bay if you feel like a very steep, 600ft (185m) walk from the parking area to the water. If not, take the right turn to Dahlet Qorrot, an old fishing harbour. There are concrete steps that lead to the upper cliff where you can walk; or try the more precarious lower path at the water's edge.

Afterwards, take the road back to Nadur, but at the first T-

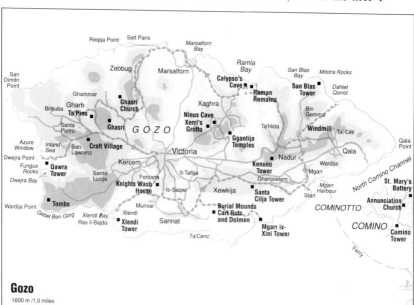

Gozo

1600 m / 1.0 miles

Making fish traps

junction go right ('Ramla'); at the second, follow 'Victoria', but at the next junction, 'Ramla' returns. Follow this road; halfway down is a small stopping place offering views into the valley below. The terraced fields are filled with fig and orange trees. Screens are made from local bamboo to protect the crops from the wind.

Ramla Bay is Gozo's longest and best beach; in the summer, stake out an early claim to be assured of space. The short cut to **Calypso's Cave** (avoiding Xaghra) is easily missed: about 100ft (30m) beyond the small police station, a steep, single-lane gravel road bears to the right. (If the short cut appears too daunting, follow the signs to Xaghra where directions to Calypso's Cave are clearly posted.) The cave is simply a narrow, rocky slit where the Siren allegedly kept Odysseus captive for seven years, but the views of Ramla Bay are excellent.

When you leave, take the main road to Xaghra, but at the first T-junction go right; the road to **Marsalforn** is well marked. Teeming with life in the summer, it is a favourite with locals and tourists alike. Swimmers have a choice between rock, shingle and sand beaches. Even at the height of the season in July and August, it is worth braving the crowds to lunch at **Otters**, family-run establishment on the water's edge. Also interesting is the fishing activity in the village. It's still a major industry here; the catch is unloaded every day and sold, often straight from the boats, from the harbour area in front of the **Calypso Hotel**.

To reach the **Salt Pans**, follow the road which runs parallel to Marsalforn's waterfront. Take the first right turn; just before the quay, a road swings left up the hill leading to the upper promenade where older homes are located. In the bay beyond the **Qbajjar Restaurant** (very popular with locals), follow the road as it leads under a sandstone cliff (water will lap at your wheels), and around the next bend

Cleaning the catch

The church at Ta'Pinu

are the salt pans, shallow pools cut from the soft coastal rock. Although Gozo now imports all the salt it needs, many people still collect it here each September.

Return to the beginning of the pans and, beyond the overhang, a right leads to **Zebbug**, a charming village strung along the top of a ridge, offering wonderful views of all Gozo. After a climb in first gear, the first flat area is the church-fronted **main square**.

For the best view over the island, leave as though heading for Victoria, but shortly after the road forks left take an immediate right, followed by a left. The road continues past a school into an area with benches and a place to park. To avoid driving through Victoria, go down the hill at the far end of the viewing area, and at the cemetery take the gravel road which branches off to the right of it. It's not signed, but eventually you'll arrive in **Ghasri**; the road at the right of the church runs through **Ghammar** to the shrine church of **Ta'Pinu**.

The area that you have travelled is not a route taken by most tourists. This is old Gozo, where farmhouses have not been prettied for tourist consumption.

Ta'Pinu is new, built between 1920 and 1936, but there has been a chapel here since the 16th century. In the late 19th century a woman is believed to have been cured after her son heard a voice in the chapel and since then many people have come to the church to ask intercession of Our Lady of Ta'Pinu. A room to the right of the Lady Chapel is filled with discarded crutches and leg braces, baby clothes and newspaper clippings, telling of miracles attributed to Ta'Pinu. The church has become world-famous, and most Gozitan weddings end with the bride putting her bouquet on the altar of the **Lady Chapel** in hope of a happy marriage.

Leaving Ta'Pinu, take the road to Victoria, then

The ornate church at Gharb

left at the **Gharb** sign. Entering the town, notice the church facade: critics are divided over this 17th-century architectural gem; some believe it's no more than a copy of Francesco Borromini's Sant'Agnes which is located on Rome's Piazza Navona, while others maintain that the work is original. Either way, the exterior is a delight to the eye. Inside, the church is smaller than expected, but it's a splendidly ornate baroque structure.

In the square, the **Market Cross** is one of the best on the island. If you're lucky, a market van will roll into town while you're there, selling everything from fruit and vegetables to chickens and rabbits, announcing its presence with a distinctive chime.

When the road from Gharb takes a right near San Lawrenz in order to get to Dwejra, look for the **Gozo Glass-blowing Centre**, which has blowers at work. The **Ta'Dbiegi Crafts Centre**, a short distance toward Dwejra, could easily be missed. Except for the excellent pottery, this is really just a collection of souvenir shops.

As you drive downhill to **Dwejra Bay**, Wied Ilma is to the left, and beyond it, the scars of the sandstone quarries. Stop near **Qawra Tower** and climb up to it for sweeping views of the bay. To the extreme left are the **Fungus Rocks**, so named because the plant which grew on them was reputed to have miraculous powers of healing; to the right is the **Azure Window** whose arch has been created by the constant pounding of water.

Paths and walkways near the shoreline change every year, the result of wind and sea erosion. The rocks are sharp and often slippery. Extreme caution is urged, as is the use of proper shoes with non-slip soles. Swimming off the rocks is possible, but wear rubber or plastic shoes.

To climb on top of the the Azure Window, take the path behind the church. Divers love exploring these rocks. The **Inland Sea** is a pool whose only outlet to the sea is through a natural tunnel; barter with the local boatmen for a sightseeing trip through it.

Down by the Azure Window

To get to **Xlendi**, Victoria cannot be avoided; fortunately, its centre can and the route is well signposted. On the Xlendi edge of Victoria on Triq Tal-ghajn, opposite Fontana Cottage Industry (lace-makers sometimes on duty) stop and look at the 17th-century **Wash-house**. From here, Xlendi is a mile or so away. Park behind the row of buildings which fronts the bay, or take the road on the left up to the apartment complexes, and park at the top of the bluff. The hillside has been landscaped down to the water, each level connected by steps and walkways. Swimming from the rocks is popular and you'll often see divers preparing for underwater explorations.

A concrete path leads back along an inlet of the bay. Cross the small bridge and walk to the **tower** on **Ras Il-Bajda**. The sandstone here is smooth enough to sunbathe comfortably and, while some of the rocks near the bay's entrance are sharp, the swimming is good. The cliffs of Gebel Ben Gorg and Wardija Point stretch toward the northwestern horizon. In the other direction, enjoy a seaside walk for several hundred yards before the path ends at the water's edge. The ambitious can hike along the clifftops to **Ta'Cenc**.

Next on this circular tour is a long sliver of water, **Mgarr Ix-Xini**, an ancient port once used by long boats and galleys for repairs and rest. To get there, and avoid Victoria, retrace your route from Xlendi as far as a concrete bus shelter where an extremely sharp right, signed **Munxar**, takes you through that town and toward **Sannat**; there, take the road which swings around the left of the church. Within a minute or so, a green-edged sign points left to Mgarr Ix-Xini. Where the hill is at its lowest, there's a road to the right. It's one-lane wide with passing places. The small natural harbour is now a fishing harbour, well off the tourist track.

To reach the last stop of the itinerary, the domed church of St John the Baptist in **Xewkija**, return to the main road, take a right and at the next T-junction turn right again (Mgarr is signed); This leads to the church, a

Cliffs at Ta'Cenc

modern building of staggering dimensions; its dome, at 243ft (75m) above the floor with a circumference of 276ft (85m), is one of the four largest in Europe. The remains of the original church, built in 1665, lie within the modern one, and are reached by a door on the left side of the main altar.

To catch the ferry back to Malta, return to the main road and follow signs to Mgarr.

Comino Island

Option 2. Cruise to Comino

Travel by boat to Comino and take a refreshing dip in the crystal clear waters of the Blue Lagoon.

—Take a ferry ride from Mgarr, or a half or full-day trip with a pleasure cruise company from other ports on the islands—

Between Malta and Gozo the tiny island of **Comino** (the name derives from *cumin* after the spice which grows wild on it) is less than a mile square and only occupied for six months in a year. There are no cars, only footpaths, and the hotel is open between Easter and the end of October. Sailing toward the island, you will first see **Comino Tower**, built in the 17th century.

If you want to go ashore for a walk, the main landing point is **Santa Marija Bay**. The small **Church of the Annunciation** is near the bay, and along the path to the tower are the remains of a Knights' quarantine hospital.

There are two sandy beaches, the largest at Santa Marija Bay, but you are sure to be tempted by a swim in the inviting waters of the **Blue Lagoon**. Located between the main island and Cominotto, a rocky islet just off-shore, you can snorkel and swim here in some of the Mediterranean's clearest waters. But be warned... most Maltese and Gozitans also recognise the beauty of this place and it can get very crowded.

Friendly ferry-man

EXCURSIONS

If there's extra time in your schedule, here are a few tours which I've enjoyed, and activities which aren't easy to organise on your own. Most organised tours depart from The Strand in Sliema or St Paul's Bay with free hotel pickups for those not staying in the immediate vicinity. A local guide who is knowledgeable about what you're seeing normally accompanies such tours. Captain Morgan Cruises, tel: 34 33 73 or 33 19 61, is the principal tour operator, but for something more personal, try a smaller company.

Cruise the Archipelago

This day-long cruise is perfect for those who want to sightsee in the easiest possible way.

Leaving Sliema, the boat sails in a clockwise direction, cruising eastward along open sea into Marsaxlokk Harbour, then south and west past the Blue Grotto, the Dingli cliffs, Golden and Anchor Bays to Comino Island. Here it anchors, a complimentary lunch is served, and time is set aside for swimming.

Later, the cruise continues along the north side of Gozo where Ramla Bay and Marsalforn are identified. Next in line are the Azure Window and Fungus Rocks of Dwejra Bay followed by Xlendi Bay and the massive cliffs of Ta'Cenc. A passage through the channel between Comino and Gozo brings you back to Malta again, and Mellieha and St Paul's bays. Malta's barren north shore soon gives way to the crowded skylines of St George's and St Julian's before re-entering Marsamxett Harbour and the home port.

Other all-day island cruises include Comino and Gozo as the sole destination, with additional stops at each island.

An Underwater Safari

This 90-minute cruise out of St Paul's Bay uses a specially designed boat which allows passengers to peer out at Malta's marine life through the 34 windows in its underwater observation keel. Even if your knowledge is only goldfish-deep, you'll walk off feeling like an expert after the specialist guide identifies each species as it darts past the boat. (A fish-feeding system assures that each cruise is accompanied by a large quantity of fish.)

Sunset and Dinner at Sea

An enjoyable, if slightly touristic, way to experience a Maltese sunset and a dinner of local barbecue specialities is to book one of the bi-weekly summer cruises. The boat heads for a secluded bay, where there's an opportunity to swim. The buffet also features complimentary wines, and afterwards there are organised party games and dancing. Others may wish to clamber on to the secluded roof for a quiet moment or three; sailing back to Sliema past a moonlit Valletta is a magical end to the cruise

The Three Cities via a 1920s Bus

Designed for those who would like to see the historical Three Cities (Cospicua, Senglea and Vittoriosa), but do not have the time to do so on their own, this delightful two-hour tour is the ideal alternative using restored buses first used in the 1920s. The only disadvantage is that no stops are made along the route.

Leaving Sliema, the bus first passes Manoel Island and the town of Ta'Xbiex (filled with embassies and elegant old homes). As you climb toward Floriana, note a British cemetery on the right. Passing through the tunnel cut through St Helen's Bastion to enter Cospicua, the cranes of the Malta Dry Docks are on your left. From here, the bus goes to the end of Senglea's 'finger' on the high centre road, then doubles back to its base along the water's edge. Touring Vittoriosa, the drive out is along the waterfront at first; returning, the bus heads inland to Victory Square, then through the Verdala Barracks and Bastion to the Margherita Lines before driving sedately back to Sliema.

(For a more detailed itinerary covering the Three Cities, see *Malta Pick & Mix Option 2, page 39*).

Down to the Seabed

Not quite an excursion, but the clear unpolluted sea surrounding the islands offers some of the best scuba diving in the Mediterranean for both Sea Card carrying expert diver and novice. Sea temperatures in the summer can go as high as 27°C (80°F) and in the winter months rarely drop below 15°C (59°F). Government-controlled dive schools assure that all international standards of safety are met. Schools hire equipment out at a nominal charge and offer novices a free introductory dive to inspire confidence and prove that being underwater is a wonderful experience.

Shopping

Malta's most traditional craft is lace-making, but Malta and Gozo are not especially famous for shopping. Valletta is the main retail centre. If you are interested in jewellery, the small side streets between Republic Street and Merchants Street are the place to go. The Savoy Shopping Centre on Republic Street offers a good range of clothes shops, mainly for young people. Malta's biggest and best organised bookshop is Sapienza at 26 Republic Street. Founded in 1905, it offers a good selection of books on Maltese topics as well as literature in foreign languages.

With a bit of luck you can buy some very nice craft products, such as lace, blown glass, ceramics, silver filigree work, weaving or knitting. Lace-making in Malta dates back to the 16th century. In the 18th century lace from Malta and Gozo was ordered for the aristrocracy from all over Europe. Today very few women have the time or inclination to take up this exacting craft. You can see it at some of the craft villages on Malta and Gozo. Many places advertise 'lace-makers at work', but when you arrive you may be told that 'it's their day off'. Try to buy smaller pieces; they are usually works of finer quality. Also available are table-cloths, napkins, place mats, collars, shawls and delicate blouses.

Blown glass is another Maltese speciality. You can watch it being made in locations on both Malta and Gozo and then buy the finished product.

Beautiful but heavy souvenirs are products made out of brass and wrought iron, for example door knockers. They come in various sizes and forms, for example in the shape of animals or mythical creatures. Very kitchy (and not very practical to carry home) are replicas of knights which are made of sheet metal. They cost about 150LM.

Pipes made of the wood of a local heather make an interesting souvenir. This particular heather grows in the higher areas in the west of the island. The famous Maltese pipes are torpedo-shaped and decorated with grotesque motifs. The pipe factory is in Marsa and is open to the public (Carrick Street; open winter 9am–4pm, summer 9am–1.30pm).

Replica knights

The factory was founded in 1930 and is owned by one of the oldest companies on Malta. Experts also value Maltese tabacco and cigars.

Unfortunately, some of the craft centres listed below are increasingly being stocked by run-of-the-mill souvenir shops, and are no longer places where the old island crafts are taught to younger people. However, unless you're lucky enough to run into someone tatting lace or working at a potter's wheel as you sightsee, these centres do offer the best opportunity to see craftspeople at work.

Craft Centres

TA'QALI CRAFTS VILLAGE
Off Valletta-Rabat Road beyond San Anton Gardens, Malta.
Tel: 41 57 86; Fax: 41 57 87
Open daily 9am–dusk. This is the largest craft centre on the islands; 15–20 companies are located on the site of a World War II airfield. Pottery, silver filigree work, glass-blowing, replica knights, weaving and knitting are among the crafts demonstrated here. The well-known Mdina Glass is also produced here, including some really exquisite glass products.

MALTA CRAFTS CENTRE
St John's Square, opposite the cathedral, Valletta
Open mid June to end September, Monday to Friday 9am–12.30pm; October to mid June, Monday to Friday 9am–12.30pm and 3–5pm. The Maltese Government craft centre exhibits and sells locally produced arts and crafts. It's also possible to obtain the addresses of craftsmen here.

PHOENICIAN GLASS BLOWERS
Manoel Island
Open Monday to Friday 9am–4pm, Saturday 9am–noon. If you enjoy watching glass blowing, this is a great place to visit. You can also buy beautiful souvenirs here – vases, paper weights, etc. There is a free boat service to Manoel from 'The Strand' in Sliema. If you can't see a boat, telephone 31 36 06 and ask for a pickup.

TA'DBIEGI CRAFTS VILLAGE
On the road to Dwejra beyond St Lawrence, Gozo.
Tel: 56 19 74; Fax: 56 03 54
Located in the former barracks. Items made of leather, wool, ceramics, glass, lace and silver are produced and sold here.

GOZO CRAFTS CENTRE AND LACE-MAKING WORKSHOP
The Citadel, Victoria
This crafts centre offers a good selection of arts and crafts produced on Gozo.

GOZO GLASS-BLOWING CENTRE
At the 'V' where the Dwejra/San Lawrenz road divides.
Tel: 56 19 74; Fax: 56 03 54
Gozo glass is typically slightly milky with a harmonious mix of colours.

FONTENELLA CRAFTS CENTRE
On the Xlendi road, opposite the old washhouse.
You can watch lace-makers at work here. Apart from lace, the souvenir shop also sells knitwear and woven products.

Open Air Markets

Valletta: Monday to Saturday until noon on Merchants' Street by St John's Square. Textiles, souvenirs, electronics, etc. Be a bit careful – many of the products are cheap imports from Asia. Sunday market is just outside City Gate, by the bus station, in St James's Ditch. This is much bigger that the weekday market, with a flea market and lots of stalls selling antiquities. The atmosphere is especially nice in the early morning.

Cospicua: Tuesday morning. A colourful market – clothes, food, household goods, etc.

Marsaxlokk: Monday to Saturday until noon around the waterfront; mainly for tourists. Sunday is when locals shop for freshly-caught fish.

Rabat: Monday to Saturday until noon. Sunday morning: lots of everything on offer.

Victoria, Gozo: Sunday morning market on Independence Square is a mecca for tourists and residents.

Eating Out

Maltese restaurants used to have a very bad name, but as lifestyles changed with increasing wealth, and thanks to the arrival of a broader selection of European visitors, new cafés and restaurants have blossomed, ready to cater for both the much-travelled Maltese (whose presence is not seasonal) and discriminating tourists.

On my first visit to Malta I was taken to Christopher's in Marsascala where I was served a meal so delicious that I still remember every dish. Over that first two-week visit, I went to others which have become favourites: Giannini, The Carriage, and The Arches on Malta, and Oleander and Gesther's on Gozo.

It is hard to find dishes which might be termed authentically Maltese. For the most part, they are a mixture of Maltese and Italian with other Continental cuisines thrown in. Fish are in abundant supply in the waters off the islands, but their presence on the menu is always subject to weather conditions.

Rabbit (*fenek*) is a favourite dish and there are farmers on the islands who specialise in breeding them for restaurants. Other specialities to look out for on local menus are *Gbejna* which is a very popular local cheese made from goat's milk; *Minestra*, a thick vegetable soup, like the Italian minestrone; another variation, *Kawlata*, is made with beans and pork. *Timpana* is a mixture of ricotta cheese, macaroni, minced meat, tomato purée, aubergines, onions and eggs encased in pastry and baked (often only two or three of the ingredients are included, and another variation is to substitute rice for the macaroni); *Torta tal-Lampuka* is made from a Mediterranean fish; the fish is sliced, then tomatoes, cauliflower, onions and olives are placed around it, everything is covered with pastry and baked. *Bragjoli* are created by mixing together meat, bacon, eggs, onions and breadcrumbs, wrapping the result in thin slices of steak and then deep-frying it.

Pastizzi is a savoury pastry stuffed with a variety of fillings, ricotta cheese, peas or meat, baked in special ovens and served hot; *Mqarets* are diamond-shaped pastry cases filled with a date mixture, then deep-fried; *Qaghaq tal-ghasel* is a ring of pastry filled with treacle and spices.

All restaurant bills include government tax. Some restaurants are beginning to follow the European custom of adding a service charge to the bill, usually between 10 and 12 percent; if it is not included, payment is at the diner's discretion.

Following are a few of my favourite places to eat, listed geographically. Unless noted, they all take major credit cards. Booking at most is necessary, especially at weekends and in summer.

Ratings: I – Inexpensive (6-7LM for two); M – Moderate (10-12LM); E – Expensive (15-20LM).

Restaurant Il Galeone, Sliema

Valletta's Bologna restaurant

Valletta

BOLOGNA
58 Republic Street
Tel: 24 61 49
Just beyond the Palace of the Grand Masters. The Maltese-Italian food is served in a dark-panelled traditional setting reminiscent of Bologna itself. Popular with business people. (E)

BRITISH HOTEL
276 St Ursula Street
Tel: 22 47 30
The hotel is not among my favourites, but its restaurant is. Book one of the balcony tables and spend lunchtime enjoying the food and watching the traffic in and out of the Grand Harbour. (M)

CAFFÉ CORDINA
244 Republic Street
Tel: 23 43 85
A Maltese institution known to locals as the 'Italian café', Caffé Cordina serves wonderful cappuccino and *ricotta pastizzi* (hot, savoury cheesecakes). They also sell traditional seasonal confections, including *Figolas* at Easter. (I)

THE CARRIAGE
Valletta Buildings
South Street
Tel: 24 78 28
Elegant restaurant on the top floor of an office block, with wonderful views. Imaginative cooking. Lunch is served Monday to Friday. Dinner Friday and Saturday. Booking essential. (E)

LA CAVE
Castille Square
Tel: 24 36 77-9
This friendly wine bar is underneath the Hotel Castille. Pastas, pizzas and salads. La Cave profits from the extensive wine list of the adjoining hotel. (I–M)

DA PIPPO TRATTORIA
136 Melitta Street
Tel: 24 19 75
This small, unpretentious restaurant with green painted tables and chairs is popular with both locals and tourists. Simple, delicious and well prepared dishes. It may get a bit crowded, so reserve a table. (M)

GIANNINI
St Michael's Bastion (off Windmill Street)
Tel: 23 71 21; Fax: 23 65 75
My favourite in the city. The bar is located on the ground floor of a patrician house; an elevator takes you two flights up to the dining rooms which overlook Marsamxett Harbour with Manoel Island and Sliema across the water. If the weather is fine, try to secure one of the five balcony tables. But the ambience and view are only part of the pleasure of dining here; the food never fails to please. Lunch is served every day, except Sunday, but dinner on Friday and Saturday only. (E)

SICILIA BAR & TAVOLA CALDA
14 St John Street/Battery Street
Tel: 24 05 69
A small restaurant with a long family tradition. Sicilian cuisine, delicious food

71

On the balcony at the British Hotel

and friendly service. Inside there's space for only 14 people but you can sit outside and enjoy a beautiful view over the Grand Harbour. Lunch only. (I)

Sliema

FORTIZZA
Tower Road
Tel: 33 69 08
Combined restaurant, pizzeria and café, located in a former British fort at Sliema Point. Friendly and lively atmosphere. (I–M)

IL GALEONE
35 Tigne Sea Front
Tel: 31 64 20
A popular, casual restaurant; Victor Bezzina is in the kitchen. Among the house specialities are *spaghetti all' arabbiata*, a starter with a very hot sauce. Booking is recommended as the restaurant is small. (M–E)

MANGAL
84 Tigne Sea Front
Tel: 34 21 74/5
I was drawn to this restaurant because the facade reminded me of a house I loved when I lived in Istanbul. The cuisine is Turkish, and several dinners later it felt that even if I was not exactly dining beside the Bosporus, I was close to it. In the summer the restaurant moves to the terrace, overlooking Marsamxett Harbour and Valletta. (M–E)

PORTOPALO RESTAURANT
30 Tigne Seafront
Tel: 33 19 15
The decor is simple, but the food good and well prepared. When ordering fish ask for the price beforehand. (M–E)

St Julian's and Paceville

BOUZOUKI
Spinola Road
Tel: 31 71 27
Long established Greek restaurant offering friendly service, a wonderful cuisine (the lamb dishes are especially delicious) and moderate prices. Relaxed atmosphere. Parking is difficult. (M)

LA DOLCE VITA
155 St George's Road
Tel: 33 70 36
A restaurant that's 'in' with the young and trendy; try for a rooftop table in summer. The trattoria-style food is very good. (E)

L'GHONELLA
Spinola Palace, Triq-il-Knisja
Romantic restaurant located in the arched cellar of the Spinola Palace (built in the late 17th century). Italian and international cuisine in elegant surroundings. Garden service in the summer. (E)

PEPPINO'S
31 St George Road
Tel: 37 32 00
This restaurant opened in 1991 and has a

wine bar on the ground floor and restaurants on the two floors above. From the second floor you can go to the terrace which offers a wonderful view over the bay. Interesting menu. (M–E)

SAN GIULIANO
Spinola Road
Tel: 33 20 00
This glass-walled restaurant overlooks Spinola Bay. Very upmarket; it's one of the places to be 'seen'. Food quality uneven. (E)

Mellieha

THE ARCHES
113 Main Street
Tel: 57 34 36
One unique feature of this elegant, spacious restaurant is its large walk-in wine cellar, a delight for wine buffs. Located centrally near the entrance to the Chapel of St Mary. Varied international menu; booking advisable. (E)

GIUSSEPPI'S
8D St Helen Street
Tel: 574882/0993579
Typically Maltese in both atmosphere and cooking and as a result very popular. The menu changes daily according to what's available in the local market. (M)

St Paul's Bay

GILLIERU
Near Bugibba
Tel: 47 34 80; 47 32 69
Family-owned for over 75 years – the fourth generation is now running this Maltese tradition. The terrace overlooks the sea and St Paul's Island; fish is a speciality. (M–E)

LUZZU
Qawra Coast Road
Tel: 57 39 25
Italian restaurant with excellent fish dishes. Situated right by the sea, with beautiful views over Salina Bay. The atmosphere is slightly 'cool'. (M)

TA'CASSIA FARMHOUSE
Qawra Road (up the hill from the JFK Memorial Garden), Qawra
Tel: 57 14 35
A converted farmhouse with rustic decor, and in the summer, a disco outdoors in the garden. (M)

Mdina

BACCHUS
Inguanez Street
Tel: 45 49 81
Elegant, expensive restaurant with international cuisine. (E)

CIAPETTI TEA GARDENS
5 St Agatha's Esplanade
Tel: 45 99 87
Situated at Bastion Square. Relaxed atmosphere and good food. (I)

FONTANELLA TEA GARDENS
Bastion Street
Tel: 45 42 64
Located directly on the city walls with wonderful views over the plateau, the Fontanella offers a large selection of Maltese cakes.

MEDINA RESTAURANT
7 Holy Cross Street
Tel: 67 40 04
In the romantic setting of one of Mdina's oldest buildings, this is among my favourite places on Malta for a long, lazy lunch (dinners also served). Stepping into the cool courtyard is like jumping back several centuries. (E)

PALAZZO COSTANZO
Villegaignon Street
Located in an old palace, this restaurant offers Maltese dishes in a historic setting. Popular with tourists. (M)

STAZZJON RESTAURANT
Mtarfa Road
Tel: 45 17 17
Underneath the city walls, in Mdina's old railway station. Authentic atmosphere and Italian-influenced cuisine. (M)

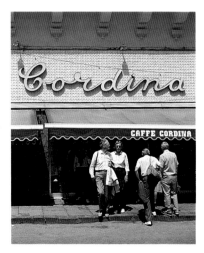

The Caffé Cordina

Seafood

Dingli

BOBBYLAND BAR & RESTAURANT
Dingli Cliffs
Tel: 45 28 95
Long established restaurant in a wonderful position over the Dingli Cliffs. The cuisine is exquisite and the service excellent. Popular with locals for an evening out and with businessmen for lunch. At weekends it might get crowded. (M–E)

Bahrija

NORTH COUNTRY BAR
Bahrija, near Rabat
Tel: 45 66 88; 45 67 63
Surely one of the best addresses if you want to enjoy rabbit Maltese style. A bit out of the way, but signposted from Rabat. Especially nice atmosphere at weekends when the locals come. The food is simple but delicious, so is the wine. (I)

Marsascala

FISHERMAN'S REST
St Thomas's Bay
Tel: 82 20 49
A very informal fish restaurant set on the edge of the ramshackle buildings on the sea front. Good, simple cooking. (I)
GABRIEL
Triq Mifsud Bonnici
Tel: 68 41 94
Gabriel enjoys a loyal clientele, which is no surprise as the fish dishes are delicious. Book ahead. Take-away service. (M)

Marsaxlokk

HUNTER'S TOWER
Triq il Kajjik
Tel: 87 17 92
Popular with locals and tourists; serves Maltese dishes, such as *Lampuka*. (M)

Gozo

Mgarr

ESPADA
Mgarr Harbour
Tel: 55 15 27
The grilled fish is perfect and Turkish cuisine good. Views over the harbour below. Upstairs is for dinner only, but light meals are served downstairs all day long. (M–E)

Marsalforn

AUBERGE TA'FRENC
Between Victoria and Marsalforn
Tel: 55 38 88
Dinners only. In a converted farmhouse, yet with an elegant atmosphere. A place to go for a special evening. (E)
OTTER'S
Triq Santa Marija
Tel: 56 24 73
Good fish, pasta and salads. Perched just above the sea with sunbeds at hand for a siesta. (I)
THE REPUBLIC
18 Triq ix-Xatt
Tel: 55 68 00
Family owned, the trattoria offers excellent and inexpensive food and friendly and fast service. Closed Mondays. (I)

Gharb

AUBERGE CHEZ AMAND
Gharb Road
Tel: 55 11 97
In an old farmhouse with views of the countryside from an elegantly appointed interior. Terraces allow outdoor dining in

Pub in Valletta

good weather. Quite expensive for Gozo, so you may want to ignore *à la carte* and try the set menu. (E)

SALVINA'S
21 Triq il-Blata
Tel: 55 25 05
The decor in Salvina's is charming, the service is great, and it's in a traditional Gozitan farming village. Closed Sundays. (M)

Xaghra

GESTHER
8th September Avenue
Tel: 55 66 21
Open for lunches only. This restaurant serves the best of simple, old fashioned home cooking. Don't miss it. (I)

OLEANDER
Victory Square
Tel: 55 72 30
One of the island's best restaurants. Good local dishes, plus wonderful fish and steaks. (I)

Xlendi

PARADISE
Mount Carmel Street
Tel: 55 68 78
Family restaurant. Excellent fish and seafood dishes. (I)

From the vine and other drinks

On my first trip to Malta, a complimentary bottle of local wine was offered with the meal; one sip and I wondered how I was going to get rid of it discreetly. Since that disastrous tasting experience, there's been a vast improvement in the quality of Malta and Gozitan wines. In particular, Marsovin Special Reserve, the Verdala reds, whites and rosés, Green Label and Citadella are good. Gozitan wine tends to be rougher.

The local brews, Farson's Strong Ale, Blue Label Ale, Cisk Lager, and Farson's Shandy, are excellent and match Continental imported lagers and beers in quality.

Two local products must be sampled: Farson's Lacto Milk-Stout and Kinnie, a slightly bitter fizzy drink. Both of these are acquired tastes but are worth trying; the Lacto Milk-Stout's label states: 'with Vitamin B for extra strength', and Kinnie is Malta's answer to Coca-Cola/root beer.

Most bars and cafés are open 9am–1am, and you can drink at any age. Children, however, are not usually welcome in public bars.

Calendar of Special Events

CARNIVAL

Malta erupts during Carnival. The merriment starts three days before Ash Wednesday and most towns and villages hold some event to mark the festivities. Valletta's celebration is the largest and its parade the longest with the most elaborate floats. Gozo's and Malta's celebrations take place over the two weekends preceding Lent.

Carnival was originally a festival to mark the end of winter; the Knights organised the first ones on Malta shortly after they arrived in 1530, but Carnival did not become an important celebration until after the Great Siege.

By the middle of the 18th century, Carnival in Valletta was in its heyday. The traditional opening was a dance called the *Parata*, a sword dance commemorating the Maltese victory over the Turks in 1565.

EASTER WEEK

Although Easter is a solemn and sombre time, visitors who come to Malta during Holy Week will find it inspiring. For the Maltese, this is both a time of sorrow and rejoicing, one whose meaning is taken seriously.

After the Palm Sunday masses and processions, Malta is quiet until Maundy Thursday. Then, the men of the parishes of St Dominic's in Valletta, the Pope Pius IX Centre in Cospicua and in Lija, open the doors of their 'Last Supper' displays.

On Thursday evenings and Fridays it is traditional to visit the seven 'Altars of Repose' erected in many churches to commemorate the Institution of the Blessed Sacrament.

There are Good Friday pageants in many towns; participants dressed in hooded robes carry life-sized statues depicting the Passion of Christ.

Saturday is a day of mourning and many restaurants, cinemas and theatres are closed. Easter Sunday is a day of great joy; church bells throughout the island peal in celebration. In the Three Cities, a statue of the Risen Christ is carried through the streets. After mass, there is the traditional Easter dinner of roast lamb.

For children, no Easter would be complete without a *Figola*, a marzipan and pastry concoction decorated with coloured icing sugar.

A 'festa' parade

can heads for Armier, a village on Malta's 'tail', where they gather with family and friends to rest and relax.

The **Feast of St Joseph the Worker** is celebrated in Valletta on May Day.

Mnarja (derived from *Luminaria*) is the popular name for the Feast of St Peter and St Paul. Held on 29 June in Rabat and Buskett Gardens, it begins with races between animals ridden bareback up Racecourse Street. It ends in the early hours after an all-night bash of food, wine, brass band music and singing.

FESTAS

The *festa* season lasts from May to September, when each of the 64 towns on Malta and the 14 on Gozo celebrates its patron saint.

All *festi* follow a similar pattern: festivities start on Friday when the saint's effigy is adorned with the treasures of the church. On Saturday morning, the local band wends its way through the streets. In the afternoon, there is a more formal parade with fireworks, balloons and banners which ends at the doors of the band club. The doors are opened, and parched throats can be soothed.

A high mass takes place on Saturday evening, then the entire village assembles in the main square for a band concert and more fireworks.

On Sunday morning fireworks announce the beginning of the saint's day, followed by a high mass, and in late morning the procession of the effigy begins. Twelve men are needed to lift and carry it, the beams resting on their shoulders.

Immediately after the parade, there is sometimes another high mass; lunch is a magnificent celebration, and the last fireworks end at midnight.

On Monday, everyone who possibly

OTHER EVENTS

February is the month of the Marathon. It started in 1986, and the 26 mile (42km) run begins in Mdina and ends in Sliema.

On 31 March, **Freedom Day** is marked with a parade in Valletta, fireworks, and races between *dghajsa* boats, whose gaily painted design is said to have originated in Phoenician times.

A **regatta** is held in the Grand Harbour on 8 September, Our Lady of Victories Day, to celebrate the victories over the Ottoman Turks in 1565 and the Axis Powers in 1945.

13 December, which celebrates Malta becoming a **Republic,** is marked by parades, band music and fireworks.

Christmas is still uncommercialised; a classic English pantomime is staged at Manoel Theatre and every family erects a nativity scene or *presepju*.

Ready to ring

77

Practical Information

GETTING THERE

By Air

Malta International Airport is near Qrendi in the southeastern part of Malta, a 15-minute drive from Valletta.

There is a bus service from the airport to Valletta, but it is unreliable and not suitable if you have a lot of luggage. It's therefore best to take one of the white taxis, buying a voucher at the arrivals terminal and presenting it to the driver.

Air Malta flies to many European and North African countries, and connects with other European carriers. Flying time from London is a little over 3 hours; from Rome, 1½ hours.

Many other airlines operate scheduled services to Malta. Charter flights are much cheaper but are usually part of a package holiday.

By Sea

Car ferries from Italy and Sicily are operated once or twice a week, summer and winter, as part of a service running to Tunisia. Drivers can bring a car on to the island for three months without a special permit but will need 'Green Card' insurance specific to Malta.

The fastest passenger ferry route to Malta from Europe is via catamaran (when the weather's favourable) from Sicily. Most travel agents can book your tickets, or contact: Virtu Rapid Ferries Office, 3 Princess Elizabeth Terrace, Ta'Xbiex. Tel: 31 88 54/5/6. Another operator is the Gozo Channel Company, tel: 55 61 14.

TRAVEL ESSENTIALS

When to Visit

April and May are delightful although the sea is not warm enough for swimming. Flowers are in full bloom, temperatures are balmy, and the crowds have not yet arrived. September and October are also great: although the flowers are not as abundant, the warm sea more than compensates. December is also pleasant; after the short rainy season, buttercups and mustard plants form a yellow carpet over much of the island. Avoid July and August when the islands are overcrowded and temperatures rise to over 40°C.

Visas and Passports

European and Commonwealth visitors require a valid passport, which entitles them to a maximum stay of three months. Visitors from former British colonies, the United States, Canada, Libya, Kuwait and Saudi Arabia have the same rights.

ary. The rainy season falls between November and March.

Clothing

In summer, bring only loose cotton clothing, avoiding synthetics. Sunglasses and a hat with a brim are essential. An extra layer is useful for evenings. Between Oc-

tober and May, always bring a rain jacket or umbrella; during winter months, add a heavy sweater and strong shoes.

Men will require a jacket for some of the more formal restaurants.

Electricity

The current is 220/240-volt and 110 for shavers; some electrical outlets require the British 3-prong flat-pin plug, while others have the round, European, two-prong plug.

Time Zones

Malta is one hour ahead of GMT and in the same time zone as Central Europe. From 31 March until the last Sunday in October, clocks are set another hour ahead.

GETTING ACQUAINTED

Geography

The Republic of Malta is located in the centre of the Mediterranean Sea. There are three inhabited islands of which Malta itself is the largest. It consists of terraced hills and rocky coast. There are no rivers and few trees. Gozo is to the northwest and has much lusher vegetation. Comino lies between Malta and Gozo.

Israelis, South Africans and some Eastern European nationals require visas. If you wish to stay longer than three months, apply to the Immigration Police Headquarters, Calcedonius Street, Floriana. Tel: 22 40 02.

Vaccinations

No inoculations are required for visitors from the United States, Canada, Australia and Europe.

Animal Quarantine

Malta is free from rabies and imposes a quarantine on all imported animals. If bringing a pet, apply first to: the Director of Agriculture, Department of Agriculture, 14 Mickel Anton Vassallo Street, Valletta, Malta. Tel: 22 49 41.

Customs

You may bring into Malta your personal effects, 200 cigarettes or 250g of other tobacco products, of which not more than 50g can be as loose tobacco, and 0.75 litre each of spirits and wine. Gifts for locals are liable to import duty.

Weather

The best months are late-April through mid-June and October when the mean daytime temperature is 25°C (75°F) and seldom goes below 13°C (56°F) at night. This is also Malta's sunniest period with an average of 10 hours of sunshine a day. The months of July and August are the hottest when temperatures can top 42°C (107°F).

In winter, snow and frosts are unknown, but it can be rainy, with harsh winds, especially in January and Febru-

Holy Trinity Anglican Church, Rudolph Street, Sliema, Tel: 33 05 75;
Union Church of Scotland and Methodist St Andrews, South Street, Valletta, Tel: 22 26 43;
Greek Orthodox Church, 83 Merchants Street, Valletta, Tel: 22 16 00;
Jewish Community Secretary, Spur Street, Valletta, Tel: 62 57 17.

Government and Economy

In September 1964, after centuries of external domination, the Maltese islands became an independent state with a parliamentary democracy. Tourism accounts for over one-fifth of Malta's gross national product. The dockyards, agriculture and manufacturing are the other industries.

Religion

Ninety-eight percent of the population of Malta have been baptised into the Roman Catholic faith. There are 364 churches on Malta and Gozo, forming the hub of village life. Women should not wear bikini or halter tops when visiting churches; men need shirts with short sleeves; and short shorts are inappropriate for both men and women. Topless and nude bathing is (officially) against the law and is punished by fines.

Catholic masses are held in the following foreign languages (check for times):

English:
St Dominic, St Dominic's Square, Rabat;
St Paul's Bay Parish Church, St Paul's Street, St Paul's Bay;
St Patrick's, St John's Bosco Street, Sliema;
St Barbara's, Republic Street, Valletta – masses also in French and German.

Italian:
St Catherine of Italy, Victory Square, Valletta.

For the non-Catholic community:
St Paul's Anglican Cathedral, West Street, Valletta, Tel: 22 47 14;

Population and Language

Malta is a melting-pot: architecture and cuisine are a mixture of North African and Southern European. The islands' mixed genetic heritage allows a *mañana* mentality to coexist with a healthy regard for the work ethic. The language (Malti) has an Arabic base, yet it's written in the Latin alphabet. English is the second language, and the vast majority of Maltese speak it well; Italian is also widely spoken.

MONEY MATTERS

Currency

The currency is the Maltese lira, occasionally referred to as the Maltese pound (written as Lm). Each lira is divided into 100 cents. Denominations are: notes: Lm2, Lm5, Lm10, Lm20, Lm50; coins: 1c, 2c, 5c, 10c, 25c, 50c, Lm1.

Credit Cards

Major credit cards are accepted everywhere, even at village street markets. Visa and Mastercard logos are seen most often, American Express less so. The American Express Card office is located at 14 Zachary Street, Valletta. Tel: 23 21 41.

Tipping

In general the Maltese do expect to be tipped. Some restaurants are now including a service charge of between 10 and 12 percent. In most cases, tipping is at the diner's discretion; 10 percent is adequate. For airport porterage, 50c; for a hotel chambermaid, Lm1 (per week). Tipping taxi drivers is not entirely necessary.

Changing Money

A small commission may be charged, and rates vary. The Bank of Valletta and the

Mid-Med Bank give competitive rates. You will need your passport for identification. Hotels may give a poorer rate of exchange but accept traveller's cheques, while shops and restaurants will take only cash (Maltese and British sterling) or credit cards.

Government regulations prohibit the import of more than Lm50, and Lm25 is the maximum you can take out. Keep all exchange receipts as they'll be needed when converting Maltese money to foreign currency.

Banking Hours

Winter: 1 October to 14 June, Monday to Friday 8.30am–12.30pm, Friday afternoon 4.30pm–6pm, Saturday 8.30am–noon. Summer: 15 June to 30 September, Monday to Friday 8am–noon also Friday 2.30pm–4pm, Saturday 8am–11.30am.

There is a 24-hour, 7-days-a-week service at the bank at Malta International airport and there are Visa card cash machines in all Bank of Valletta branches and tourist resorts. Tourist Information centres throughout the islands have a pamphlet with the opening hours of all bank branches.

GETTING AROUND

The Maltese are erratic drivers. Traffic regulations and traffic lights are routinely ignored. Speed limits are 40mph/64kph on highways and 25mph/40kph in built-up areas, but no one obeys them.

Parking is another headache. It can be difficult to find a space and police are fastidious about illegal parking.

So is it worth renting a car on Malta? On balance, yes (although the old, rambling buses run frequently all over the island and can be fun). Driving gives you a freedom that buses will not, and using taxis all the time works out expensive. But drive defensively, go with the flow and, above all, don't try to be smart.

To hire a car you need only your national driving licence.

The cost of fuel is on a par with Britain and the Continent (expensive by American standards) but most types of hired car are economical. Petrol stations are generally open 7am–6pm, but be sure to fill up for the weekend by noon on Saturday as stations close on Sundays and public holidays.

Car Hire

Most large European and American car hire firms are on the island; in summer book in advance. You must be 25 years of age (or 21 if you pay for fully comprehensive insurance), and produce either a valid driving licence or an international driver's permit. Many car rental firms also offer a selection of chauffeur-driven cars.

INTER RENT EUROPCAR
Malta International Airport and, through their licensee, John's Garage at 38 Villambrosa Street, Hamrun.
Tel: 23 87 45.
AVIS RENT-A-CAR
59 Msida Seafront
Tel: 22 59 86.
WEMBLEY'S RENT-A-CAR
50 St George's Road, St Julian's. Tel:
37 41 41;
37 42 42;
33 66 49.

St Andrew's Road, St Andrew's
Tel: 33 20 74.
GOZO UNITED RENT-A-CAR
5 Xaghra Road, Victoria
Tel: 55 37 36.

Taxis

Taxis are usually white Mercedes, and can be picked up at the various taxi ranks, the airport, harbours and outside hotels. It is wise to insist that either the meter be switched on, or make sure you agree a price before you start your jouney.

Buses

Since so many local people depend upon the buses, the system is both reliable and inexpensive. On Malta, the main bus station is just outside the city gates of Valletta and most routes terminate here. Fares are calculated according to zones, but never cost more than a few cents. Services begin at about 5.30am and stop at around 10pm on weekdays and 11pm on weekends. For bus information in Malta, call 22 59 16. On Gozo services are less frequent; the main bus station is in Victoria, on Triq Putirjal (tel: 55 60 11).

Water Transport

A car and passenger ferry operates between Cirkewwa on Malta and Mgarr Harbour on Gozo, daily from 5.30am (7am from Cirkewwa) offering up to 21 return crossings daily; travel time is about 25 minutes. During summer, services continue into the night and there is a non-stop shuttle service during peak holiday periods.

During the peak season, a passenger catamaran sails between Mgarr and Marsalforn on Gozo, and between Sliema and Bugibba on Malta.

For more detailed information contact: the Gozo Channel Co, at Mgarr (Gozo): tel: 55 61 14 or 56 16 22. At Cirkewwa (Malta): tel: 58 04 35 or 57 18 84.

To get to Comino, the Comino Hotel runs a ferry service to Cirkewwa. Contact the Comino Hotel, tel: 52 98 21 for further details.

A day-time passenger ferry operates across Marsamxett between The Strand in Sliema and the foot of St Mark's Street in Valletta between April and November. Crossing time is 5 minutes.

Helicopter

A helicopter service makes up to nine flights a day in the summer to the airfield opposite the Gozo Experience. Tel: 88 29 20/5 (Malta Airport) or 55 79 05/56 13 01 (Gozo Heliport) for details.

Bicycles and Motorcycles

Helmets are required by law for drivers and passengers. Stay out of the cities, where cyclists have a very low rating. Below are a few hire shops:

CYCLE STORE
135 Eucharistic Congress Street, Mosta. Tel: 43 28 90. Bicycles only.
VICTOR SULTANA
New Building, Main Gate Street, Victoria, Gozo. Tel: 55 64 14

Motorcycles only:
L'ARONDE FRANK GALEA
Upper Gardens, St Julian's
Tel: 37 07 65
PETER'S SCOOTER SHOP
175A D'Argens Road, Msida
Tel: 33 52 44
ALBERT'S SCOOTER SHOP
216/6 Rue D'Argens, Gzira
Tel: 34 01 49
Also a branch at 22 Upper St Albert Street.

Carriages

Looked upon as a quaint way to see Valletta or Mdina, the *karozzin* were once Malta's primary mode of transportation. Prices vary (about Lm5–10 for half an hour for two people). To avoid any disputes, it's best to agree the price before setting out.

On Foot

Malta and Gozo are great places for walkers. *Landscapes of Malta* (Sunflower Books) is an excellent guide for exploring by foot (but check you have an up-to-date edition).

Maps

The map in the wallet at the back of this guide plots all the routes described in this book. It is also detailed enough for exploring independently.

Other good maps include *Bartholomew Clyde Leisure Map of Malta and Gozo* (also shows bus routes), *The A to Z Guide to the Streets of Malta* by A Attard Francis, the *Tourist Atlas of the Maltese Islands*, and the 1:25,000 map series published by the mapping unit of the Works Department (*West Malta*; *East Malta*; *Gozo/Comino*).

In addition, the tourist office, many hotels and other commercial organisations will supply free maps to visitors on request.

HOURS & HOLIDAYS

Business Hours

Malta takes a siesta 12.30–3.30pm (until 4 or 4.30pm in the summer). Businesses generally open between 8.30am–5pm although in summer government offices (and some businesses) open only 7am–1pm. Shops usually open 9.30am–12.30pm and from 3pm (4pm summer) to 7 or 8pm.

Public Holidays

New Year's Day:	1 January
St Paul's Day:	10 February
St Joseph's Day:	19 March
Freedom Day:	31 March
Good Friday	
Workers' Day:	1 May
'Sette Giugno':	7 June
Saints Peter and Paul:	29 June
Assumption:	15 August
Victory Day:	8 September
Independence Day:	21 September
Feast of the Immaculate Conception:	8 December
Republic Day:	13 December
Christmas Day:	25 December

ACCOMMODATION

Hotels are rated according to international standards and classified from one to five stars. My favourites are:

Malta

CASTILLE***
Castille Square, Valletta
Tel: 24 36 77
Just within the city walls, across the street from the Auberge de Castille, the Prime Minister's office.

LE MERIDIEN PHOENICIA****
The Mall, Floriana
Tel: 22 52 41
Just outside the city gates of Valletta. A Forte Group hotel. Pool. Secretarial services available. Conference facilities.

FORTINA****
Tigne Sea Front, Sliema
Tel: 34 33 80
The best situated hotel on the island. On the waterfront, minutes from shopping streets and facing across the harbour towards Valletta. Excellent pool and gym.

PARK HOTEL****
Graham Street, Sliema
Tel: 34 37 80/2
Situated just off Tower Road, this is a haven for the traveller on a tight budget. Every room contains a kitchenette with crockery and cutlery. Restaurant and roof pool with a great view.

HOWARD JOHNSON DIPLOMAT****
173 Tower Road, Sliema
Tel: 34 53 61/6
Mid-priced hotel, directly across from the rocky beach. 111 rooms, comfortable and practically furnished, 2 suites. Big breakfast menu, bars, a cafeteria, two restaurants, conference rooms and a roof-top swimming pool make this hotel popular with tour operators.

ASTORIA*
46 Point Street, Sliema
Tel: 33 20 89
Children-friendly, small hotel with only 20 beds, near the coastal road.

CORINTHIA SAN GORG****
St George's Bay, St Julian's
Tel: 37 41 14/6
Opened in 1995, this is one of the Corinthia Group's flagship hotels. Good location and with excellent facilities that include a wide choice of restaurants. On its own beach resort and with a well-appointed lido. Business centre and executive suites.

HILTON INTERNATIONAL****
St Julian's
Tel: 33 62 01/9
Luxurious hotel in quiet location, situated on a rocky plateau by the sea. There are three pools, a nightclub and tennis courts. Five minutes walk to the centre of St Julian's and 500 metres to the casino. Mainly British guests come here.

LION COURT**
9 Nursing Sisters Street, St Julian's
Tel: 33 62 51/2
The Lion Court is very family orientated and situated a little bit away from the coastal road. The 16 rooms are practically furnished.

Gozo's Hotel Cornucopia

GILLIERU HARBOUR****
Church Square, St.Paul's Bay
Tel: 57 27 20
Nice hotel (50 rooms) in quiet location and with an excellent restaurant. The Gillieru has its own diving school.

SUNCREST****
Qawra Coast Road, Qawra, St Paul's Bay
Tel: 57 71 01
Huge and modern hotel with 413 rooms at the Salina Bay. Several restaurants, bars, a disco and good sports facilities make the Suncrest popular.

CORINTHIA MISTRA VILLAGE CLUBHOTEL
Xemxija Hill, St Paul's Bay
Tel: 58 04 81
Holiday resort situated on a hill over the St Paul's Bay. Wonderful views over the Xemxija Bay on the one side and over the Mistra Valley on the other side. The apartments are individually decorated and

have up to three bedrooms. There are restaurants but you can also prepare your own meals. All guests can enjoy the facilities at Mistra Sports Centre, with tennis and squash courts, a diving school, swimming pools and fitness rooms. Activity programme for children.

MERCURE SELMUN PALACE****
Selmun, Mellieha
Tel: 52 10 40
House belonging to Air Malta and the German Maritim Group, located on the hill between St. Paul's Bay and Mellieha Bay. Wonderful views over the island. The old castle Selmun is integrated into the hotel complex. 148 rooms.

RAMLA BAY RESORT****
Rambla Bay, Marfa
Tel: 52 21 81/3
Well situated hotel with 64 rooms, restaurant, bars, minigolf and watersports.

CORINTHIA PALACE HOTEL*****
De Paule Avenue, San Anton
Tel: 44 03 01
Corinthia Palace offers all the luxury of a 5-star hotel with 158 elegantly furnished rooms. The breakfast buffet is magnificent. In the courtyard you'll find the 'Athenaeum', a health and beauty centre. Corinthia Palace is located near San Anton's Gardens in the middle of the island, but there is a free bus transfer to Sliema, Valletta and to the golf course in Marsa.

GROSVENOR***
Pope Alexander VII Junction, Balzan
Tel: 48 69 16
Quiet and ideal for those who can live without nightly entertainment. There are 75 rooms, a pool, a restaurant and a bar.

GRAND HOTEL VERDALA****
Inguanez Street, Rabat
Tel: 64 17 00
Lovely location, within walking distance

of Mdina. Beach-lovers would not be happy here, but the pools are great and the views terrific. (At the time of writing, it was closed for major refurbishment.)

XARA PALACE**
St Paul's Square, Mdina
Tel: 45 05 60
Located in an old palace next to the city walls. Simple, but very romantic. 18 rooms, restaurant, bar and a terrace.

Gozo

CORNUCOPIA***
Gnien Imrek, Xaghra
Tel: 55 64 86
A small, family-run hotel. A good kitchen, friendly staff and an excellent wine list.

TA'CENC****
Sannat
Tel: 55 68 30
Ambience and service are delightful. In a tranquil location, its single-storey buildings are grouped around the two pools. Access to a rocky beach down a steep hill.

L'IMGARR*****
Mgarr
Tel: 56 04 55/7
This luxury hotel built in Gozo farmhouse style is one of the best hotels on the Maltese Islands. It is located near the ferry terminal, has 74 very elegant rooms and some suites. The prize-winning restaurant is excellent. A special feature of the hotel is the glass lift leading from the reception to the upper floors which are built like galleries around the middle.

Country houses: Popular on Gozo are old farmhouses turned into holiday homes. Some are new, but built and furnished in the old style. They are made of island stone, and are rustic and cosy; some have terraces. You can also book a housekeeper to do the cooking, cleaning and shopping for you. Country houses can be booked from all major travel agencies.

Comino

THE COMINO****
Tel: 52 98 21/9
Gozo is a 15-minute boat ride away. Ten-

nis and water sports; or you can hike around the 1sq mile (2½sq km) of the island. Open Easter to end October only (*see page 65*); fills up early in the year.

Health Matters

Most well-known medicines are available in Malta but bring your own if you have a specific problem.

Bring insect repellent creams and sprays; beware of jellyfish which are sometimes found offshore. In some places it is wise to wear rubber shoes in the sea.

Tap water is safe to drink, but avoid water in fountains.

Take precautions, even in winter, when sun-bathing. Use a high SPF factor suncream or total sun-block for the first few days, and change to a lower rated suncream when you have acclimatised. You can find most popular brands in shops and pharmacies.

Pharmacies

Notoriously difficult to find because they carry no recognisable symbol, opening hours generally range from 8.30 or 9am until 1pm and 3.30–7pm. Look in the *Malta Times* for those open over the weekend.

The UK, Belgium, the Czech and Slovak Republics, Australia, Poland, Cyprus, Spain, Greece, Hungary, Tunisia, Turkey

and Italy have reciprocal health agreements with Malta. Otherwise, make sure you are adequately insured. All doctors and dentists on Malta and Gozo speak English and probably Italian.

Emergency Services

Ambulance/emergency service:
Malta, *tel: 196*
Gozo, *tel: 56 16 00*
ST LUKE'S HOSPITAL
Gwardamangia, near Valletta
Tel: 24 12 51, 23 41 01
Malta's main hospital.
CRAIG HOSPITAL
Ghin Qatet Street, Victoria
Tel: 56 16 00
The only hospital on Gozo.

Safety

Malta is still a comparatively safe place for tourists and a lone woman can feel secure in most places at night, but use common sense.

Don't leave money or valuables on the beach while you swim; don't carry large amounts of cash on you. Many hotels offer safety boxes for guests' valuables.

The only known black spot is the parking area at Peter's Pool on Delimara Peninsula. In case of theft or attack, notify the police immediately and, if necessary, seek assistance from your embassy.

Police

MALTA POLICE HEADQUARTERS
Calcedonius St, Floriana
Tel: 22 40 01/02
GOZO POLICE HEADQUARTERS
113 Republic Street, Victoria
Tel: 56 20 46/8
Emergency numbers:
Malta, *tel: 191*
Gozo, *tel: 56 20 40*

Illicit Drugs

Don't even think about it. The conservative Maltese impose stiff penalties.

Complaints

The Malta Tourism Authority (*see page 91*) will deal with any serious complaints which you cannot settle personally.

Inside the Manoel Theatre

International dialling codes:
Denmark: 0045
France: 0033
Germany: 0049
Netherlands: 0031
Norway: 0047
Ireland: 00353
Italy: 0039
Spain: 0034
Sweden: 0046
UK: 0044
US/Canada: 001

COMMUNICATIONS & NEWS
Postal Services

Post offices in most towns and villages open from 7.45am–1pm, Monday–Saturday. In Valletta and Victoria on Gozo, the main post offices stay open until 6pm and 5.15pm respectively. You can buy stamps from newsagents, hotels and some souvenir shops. The letter-boxes are red, like British ones. Postcards or letters to European countries cost 16c.

MAIN POST OFFICE, MALTA
Auberge d'Italia, Merchants Street, Valletta
MAIN POST OFFICE, GOZO
129 Republic Street, Victoria

Telephone & Fax

The telephone system has been upgraded to include the Internet, e-mail etc. It is now possible to dial any country on the international direct dialling system if you know the prefix.

Use call-boxes for local calls; they take phone cards or 5c coins. For international directory enquiries, dial 190. For operator assistance in Malta, dial 194; on Gozo, dial 894.

Local and long-distance calls and faxes may be sent from Maltacom offices at: Malta International Airport, tel: 22 58 61. Valletta: South Street, tel: 24 14 09 or 22 41 31. Sliema: Bisazza Street, tel: 33 39 52. St Julian's: St George's Road, tel: 33 82 21. St Paul's Bay: Paul's Street, tel: 57 72 88. Qawra: Fliegu Street, tel: 57 66 03. Gozo: Republic Street, Victoria, tel: 56 39 90.

Media

The Times, one of Malta's two English-language daily papers, is the best source of information about current events.

Most of the major European daily papers are delivered on the afternoon of publication; periodicals a day later. (On Gozo, the schedule is a day later for newspapers and periodicals.)

The national broadcasting company of Malta is TVM. It and five independent TV stations air local programmes in Maltese and English plus an assortment of American, Australian and British offerings. Most Italian TV broadcasts reach the Maltese islands.

Malta has cable TV and most hotels catering to tourists are wired for SkyNews, CNN, and selected British, French and German channels.

Radio Malta 1 (999khz medium wave) has local news and music. Radio Malta 2 (93.7VHF/FM) plays popular music; both of these broadcast in Maltese only. There are about a score of commercial radio stations, three of which broadcast in English. Check the local newspapers.

USEFUL INFORMATION
Nightlife

Paceville and St Julian's are where most of Malta's year-round nightlife happens. But in the summer, discos thump away in all Malta's resort areas.

Discos

AXIS
St George's Road, St Julian's
Tel: 31 80 78
EUPHORIA
St George's Bay, St Julian's
Tel: 34 11 91
LA GROTTA
Xlendi Road (towards Victoria), Xlendi
Tel: 55 15 83
Set in a vast cave suspended above a flood-lit ravine. The prettiest nightclub in the Maltese islands with inside and outside dance floors. Daily except October to May weekends only, from 9pm.

Gambling

The Maltese enthusiastically participate in their weekly Lotto; foreigners and locals compete for large prizes in the National Lottery. A new scheme now offers prizes in foreign currency.

MHUX PERMESS TGHUM JEW TIXXEMMEX
'TOPLESS' JEW GHARWIEN
NO NUDE OR TOPLESS SWIMMING AND
SUNBATHING
È VIETATO NUOTARE NUDI, 'TOPLESS' O
ABBRONZARE SENZA COSTUME DA BAGNO
NUDISME ET SEINS NUS INTERDITS
SUR LA PLAGE ET PENDANT LA BAIGNADE
OBEN OHNE BADEN UND SONNEN NICHT
ERLAUBT
SE PROHIBE BAÑARSE DESNUDOS,
'TOPLESS' O TOMAR EL SOL SIN BAÑADOR

THE CASINO AT DRAGONARA
Paceville
Tel: 31 28 88
Black Jack, roulette, *chemin de fer* or slot machines. Jacket and tie required.
ORACLE CASINO
New Dolmen Hotel, Bugibba
Tel: 58 15 10
Fax: 58 58 18
Opened in 1998.

Facilities for the Disabled

Despite efforts by hoteliers and others in the tourist industry, it's still difficult to sightsee in Malta if you're physically disabled. The terrain of the cities makes it difficult to navigate a wheelchair.

For information regarding facilities contact: the Health Education Unit, tel: 22 40 71 or the National Commission for the Handicapped, tel: 48 77 89.

Students

NSTS
(Student and Youth Travel Organisation)
220 St Paul's Street, Valletta
Tel: 24 99 83; 24 66 28

and *45 St Francis Square, Victoria, Gozo*
Tel: 55 39 77
An invaluable booklet, the *Student Saver Discount Scheme*, lists shops, exhibitions, restaurants and transport offering discounts to those with an ISIC (International Student Identity Card).

The Arts

The season runs from October to May. Many events are staged at Manoel Theatre; check *The Times* for times.
MANOEL THEATRE
Old Theatre Street
Tel: 24 63 89 for booking enquiries.
One of the oldest theatres still in use in Europe. Tours of the theatre at 10.45am and 11.30am Monday–Friday, 11.30am Saturday, summer and winter.
ASTRA THEATRE
Republic Street, Victoria, Gozo

Children

There are few facilities especially designed for youngsters (Malta and Gozo aren't ideal for children), but Popeye Village and Rinella Movie Park should keep them amused for a few hours. For the best sandy beaches, base yourself close to Mellieha or Golden Bay. The most child-friendly spot is White Rocks, home to Splash & Fun Waterpark, Mediterraneo Marine World and a dinosaur theme park.

Gay Scene

No contact magazine or hotline exists for the gay community. There are clubs which welcome gays and lesbians, but their popularity changes with the seasons. Best to check in your local community. The age of consent on Malta is 18.

Nude Bathing

Nude bathing for all and topless bathing for women is prohibited, though it is practised on some beaches. A fine, jail or deportation can result if prosecuted.

KEY ATTRACTIONS

All museums and temple sites are run by the government and, unless otherwise indicated, keep to the following opening times: winter (1 October to 15 June): Monday to Saturday 8.15am–5pm Sunday 8.15am–4pm (sometimes with 2-hour closing for lunch); summer (16 June to 30 September): Monday to Saturday 7.45am–2pm. Opening hours for churches vary, but in general they are 8–12.30pm and 3.30–7pm; tourists are asked to refrain from sightseeing during services.

Valletta

NATIONAL MUSEUM OF ARCHAEOLOGY
Republic Street, Tel: 23 77 30
Housed in the Auberge de Provence, megalithic pottery, sculpture, etc. from Malta's temples and prehistoric sites.

NATIONAL MUSEUM OF FINE ARTS
South Street, Tel: 22 57 69
Works by Italian masters and Maltese artists.

NATIONAL WAR MUSEUM
Fort St Elmo at end of Republic Street
Tel: 22 24 30
World War II items and the story of Malta's second siege.

PALACE OF THE GRAND MASTERS
Republic Street
Tel: 22 12 21
The original Magisterial Palace of the Knights, now the office of the President and also the House of Representatives.

ST JOHN'S CO-CATHEDRAL
St John's Square, between Republic and Merchants streets
Tel: 22 05 36; 22 56 39; 24 44 76
Designed by Maltese architect Gerolamo Cassar in 1577, the cathedral contains

frescoes by Calabrian artist Mattia Preti and Caravaggio's *The Beheading of St John*. Open: Monday to Friday 9.30am–12.45pm and 1.30–5.15pm, Saturday 9.30am–12.40pm and 4–5pm. Museum open: Monday to Friday 9.30am–12.30pm and 1.30–4.30pm, Saturday 9.30am–12.30pm.

Other churches worth visiting in Valletta include: St Paul Shipwreck, St Paul Street; St Paul's Anglican Cathedral, West Street; The Carmelite Church, Old Theatre Street; St Barbara's Church, Republic Street; The Church of Our Lady the Victories, Ordinance Street and St Dominic's Orator.

THE MEDITERRANEAN CONFERENCE CENTRE
North end of Merchants Street
Tel: 24 38 40/6; 24 37 76
The Malta Experience, a 40-minute audio-visual, is shown here hourly from 11am–4pm Monday to Friday, 11am, noon and 3pm Saturday, Sunday and holidays.

Mdina

MDINA DUNGEON
First right after entering city gates
Tel: 45 02 67
The fascinating story of torture from the time of St Paul. Diagrams, sound tracks and suitably scary figures. Located in actual dungeons. Open: June to September, daily 10am–7pm; October to May 10am–6pm.

MDINA CATHEDRAL AND CATHEDRAL MUSEUM
St Paul's Square
Tel: 45 46 97; 45 41 36; 45 66 20
A baroque masterpiece, with paintings, and engravings by Dürer, Rembrandt, Piranesi and Van Dyck. Open: Monday to

Saturday 9am–5pm. Mass: Monday to Saturday at 7.45am, 9am and 6pm; Sunday at 7, 8, 9.30, 11am and 6pm. Museum open: October to May, Monday to Saturday 9am–1pm and 1.30pm–4.30pm; June to September, Monday to Saturday 9am–1pm and 1.30pm–5pm.

NATIONAL MUSEUM OF NATURAL HISTORY
St Publius Square
Tel: 45 59 51
Worth visiting if only for the tour of the Vilhena Palace.

Rabat

ST PAUL'S CHURCH AND GROTTO
Tel: 45 44 67
St Paul's is Rabat's original parish church. The Grotto is reputed to be where St Paul lived following his shipwreck in AD60.

ROMAN VILLA AND MUSEUM
Museum Esplanade
Tel: 45 41 25
Remains of a wealthy nobleman's home. Highlights include remarkable mosaic floors, pottery and grand columns.

THE CATACOMBS
Three Christian catacombs from AD50.

TARXIEN PREHISTORIC TEMPLES
Old Temples Street, Tarxien
Tel: 22 55 78
Pagan temples dating back to the third and fourth millennia BC.

THE HYPOGEUM
Burial Street between Paola and Tarxien
Tel: 82 55 79
Underground network of burial chambers scheduled to reopen in 2000 following years of restoration.

HAGAR QIM AND MNAJDRA
Near Zurrieq
Temples dating from the late megalithic period.

GHAR DALAM CAVE
At Birzebbuga, Tel: 82 44 19
Fossilised remains of animals.

BORG IN-NADUR
Near Birzebbuga
A fortified village from around 1500BC.

USEFUL ADDRESSES

Malta Tourism Offices Abroad

UNITED KINGDOM
Malta Tourism Authority
Malta House, 36 Piccadilly,
London W1V 0PP
Tel: (020) 7292 4900
Fax: (020) 7734 1880

NETHERLANDS
Nationaal Verdeersbureau Malta
Geelvinck Building, 4th Floor,
Singel 540, 1017 AZ, Amsterdam
Tel: (020) 20 72 23

GERMANY
Fremdenverkehrsamt Malta
Schilerstrasse 30–40, D-60313,
Frankfurt am Main 1
Tel: (069) 28 58 90

FRANCE
Office National du Tourisme de Malte
9 Cité de Trevise,
75009 Paris
Tel: 01 48 00 03 79

ITALY
Ente Nazionale per il Turismo di Malta
Via M. Gonzaga 7, 20123 Milano
Tel: (02) 86 73 59

UNITED STATES

Malta National Tourist Office
Empire State Building, Suite 4412,
New York, NY 10018, USA
Tel: (212) 695 9520

Alternatively, www.searchmalta.com has all kinds of information on Malta.

Tourist Offices within Malta

MALTA TOURISM AUTHORITY
280 Republic Street
Valletta
Tel: 22 44 44; 22 44 45
Fax: 22 04 01
www.visitmalta.com
email: info@visitmalta.com
This office is not open to personal callers. For walk-in information, use the following offices.

Malta
1 City Gate, Valletta
Tel: 23 77 47
Arrivals Lounge, Malta International Airport
Tel: 69 99 60 73/4
Balluta Bay, St Julian's
Tel: 34 26 71/2

Gozo
Independence Square, Victoria
Tel: 56 14 19
Mgarr Harbour, Gozo
Tel: 55 33 43; 55 81 06

Air Malta Offices

285 Republic Street, Valletta
Tel: 22 12 07; 23 68 19; 23 70 41
Tower Road, Sliema
Tel: 33 06 46; 31 62 42
Enquiries at Malta International Airport:
Tel: 24 96 00; 69 78 00; 88 29 16/17
www.airmalta.com

Embassies and Consulates

AMERICAN EMBASSY
Development House,
St Anne Street, Floriana
Tel: 23 59 61/5
AUSTRALIAN HIGH COMMISSION
Ta'Xbiex Terrace, Ta'Xbiex
Tel: 33 82 01/5
BRITISH HIGH COMMISSION
7 Anne Street, Floriana
Tel: 23 31 34/7

FRENCH EMBASSY
Villa Seminia
12 Sir Temi Zammit Street
Ta'Xbiex
Tel: 33 11 07; 33 58 56
GERMAN EMBASSY
Il-Piazzetta, Entrance B,
Tower Road, Sliema SLM 16
Tel: 33 65 31; 33 39 76
ITALIAN EMBASSY
5 Vilhena Street, Floriana
Tel: 23 31 57/8; 23 02 65/6
SPANISH EMBASSY
145/10, Tower Road, Sliema
Tel: 31 41 64/5

FURTHER READING

History

Abela, A, *Malta: A Panoramic History*
Blouet, B, *The Story of Malta*. London, 1967 (Malta, 1993).
Bradford, Ernle, *The Siege of Malta*. Penguin.
Bridge, Antony, *The Crusades*. Granada.
Hogan, George, *Malta: The Triumphant Years 1940–4*. Robert Hale.

Art and Architecture

Buhagiar, Mario, *Iconography of the Maltese Islands 1400–1900*.
Hughes, Quentin, *The Buildings of Malta 1530–1795*. London, 1967.
Hughes, Quentin, *Malta: A Guide to the Fortifications*. Malta, 1993.
Mahoney, Leonard, *5000 Years of Architecture in Malta*. Malta, 1996.
de Piro, Nicholas, *International Dictionary of Artists Who Painted Malta*.

Other

Apa Publications, *Insight Guide: Malta*. London, 1999. Detailed run-down of the sights, plus background essays, stunning photography and a fact-packed Travel Tips.
Caruana Galizia, Anne and Helen, *Recipes from Malta*. Progress Press, Malta.
Cassar-Pullicino, Joseph, *Studies in Maltese Folklore*. Malta University Publications.
Eco, Umberto, *Foucault's Pendulum*. Secker & Warburg.
Gerada-Azzopardi, Eric, *Malta Revisited*

A

Acre 11
Agatha, St 29, 30, 32
Algardi, Alessandro 22
Arabs 11, 17, 54
Armier 51
Azure Window (Gozo) 63, 66

B

Bahrija 74
Belisarius 17, 44
Birgu (Vittoriosa) 12, 31, 39, 41
Birkirkara 38
Birzebbuga 44
Blue Grotto 47, 66
Boffa, Sir Paul 28
Bonnici, Giuseppe 21
Borg in-Nadur 19, 44
Bormla (Cospicua) 39
Bouillon, Godfrey de 11, 33
British 13, 14, 17, 54
Bush, George 19, 44

C

Cachia, Domenico 38, 50
Calypso 54
Calypso's Cave (Gozo) 61
carnival 76
Carthaginians 10, 17
Casino 52
Cassar, Gerolama 13, 22 26, 30, 48
Charles v 12
Churchill, Winston 15
Cirkewwa 67
Clapham Junction 49
Comino Island 65, 66, 67

Condé 13
Constantinople 12, 17
Cospicua 27, 39, 41, 67, 69
Cottoner, Grand Master 27
crafts 37, 58, 63, 68–9
cruises 32, 47, 65, 66–7
Cyprus 11

D

Dahlet ix Xilep 51
Dahlet Qorrot (Gozo) 63, 66
Delimara 45
Dimech, Manuel 28
Dingli 49, 66, 74
Dingli, Tomasso 38
dockyards 18, 35, 40, 67

E

Easter week 76
Eisenhower, General 16
Elizabeth ii, Queen 27
Erardi, Stefano 29

F

Fenech Adami, Dr Eddie 17
Ferdinand of Aragon 11, 12
festivals 38, 48, 51, 76–7
Filfla Island 48
Firenzuloa, Marculano da 39
Floriana 67
Fort Ricasoli 35, 43
Fort St Angelo 35, 39, 42
Fort St Elmo 12, 13, 21, 27, 35, 39
Fort St Michael 35, 39
French 13, 14, 17, 54
Fungus Rocks (Gozo) 63, 66

G

Gafa, Lorenzo 29, 32, 57
gardens 25, 27, 28, 36, 40, 48
Genga, Bartolomeo 42
George Cross 15, 17, 23, 27
George VI, King 15, 16, 23
Germans 15
Ggantija (Gozo) 17, 22, 59
Ghammar (Gozo) 62
Gharb (Gozo) 63, 74–5
Ghasri (Gozo) 62
Golden Bay 51
Gorbachev, Mikhail 17, 44
Gozo 10, 14, 17, 54–65, 74–5
    history 54
Gozo Heritage 59
Grand Harbour 10, 34, 35
Great Siege 12, 17, 23, 35, 39, 41, 76
Greeks 12

H, I

Hagar Qim 10, 17, 22, 47
Hompesch, Ferdinand de 13
hotels 83–6
Il-Ghadira Beach 51
Inquisitor's Palace (Vittoriosa) 43
Invicta 12
Isabella of Castile 11, 12
Isla (Senglea) 39
Italy 15
Ittar, Stefano 23

K, L

Kahlil, Sultan 11
Kalkara 43
Knights of St John of Jerusalem 11, 12,
    13, 14, 17, 22, 23, 24, 26, 27, 28, 31,
    35, 41, 42, 54, 65, 76
language 11, 17
Laparelli, Francesco 13
Lascaris, Grand Master 28
Louis XVI, King 13
Ludwig of Sicily 17
Lybia 10

M

Malta, British Crown Colony 14
    Great Siege
    history 10–17
    Independence 16
    World War II 15

Malta Experience 27
Manno, Vincenzo and Antonio 33
Manoel Island 25, 34, 67, 69
marathon 77
Marfa Ridge 51
markets 44, 69
Marsalforn (Gozo) 54, 59, 61, 66, 74
Marsamxett Harbour 25, 26, 34, 35, 66
Marsascala 46, 70, 74
Marsaxlokk 17, 24, 44, 66, 69, 74
Mazzuoli, Giuseppe 22
Mdina 14, 17, 22, 29–34, 73
    Dungeons 32
    Cathedral of St Paul 32, 73
Mdina Experience 32
Mediterranean Sea 10
Mellieha 50, 66, 73
Mgarr Ix-Xini (Gozo) 64, 74
Mintoff, Dom 16
Mnajdra 10, 17, 22, 47
Mosta 37–8
Mqabba 47
Munxar (Gozo) 64
museums 21, 22, 32, 33, 38, 42, 58
Mussolini 15

N, O

Nadur (Gozo) 60
Napoleon 13, 14, 17
National Museum of Fine Arts (Valletta) 21
Odysseus 54, 61

P, Q

Paceville 52, 72–3
Parisot de Valette, Jean 12
Paul I, Tsar 13
Paul, St 11, 17, 29, 30, 32, 33, 50
Perellos, Grand Master Ramon 24, 25
Peter's Pool 45
Phoenicians 17, 54
Pius VII, Pope 22
Pius X, Pope 38
Poggo, Antonio Manuele 58
Popeye Village 51
Preti, Mattia 22, 29, 33, 56
Publius 11, 17, 32
Qala (Gozo) 60
quarries 47

R

Rabat 20–30, 69
Ramla Bay (Gozo) 61, 66

Ras il-Qammieh 51
Red Tower 51
regatta 77
restaurants 25, 30, 34, 46, 49, 51, 52, 59, 61, 70–5
Rhodes 11
Richard the Lionheart 11
Roger the Norman, Count 11, 17, 32
Rohan-Polduc, de 13
Romans 10, 17, 54
Rommel 15
Roosevelt, Franklin Delano 23
Russians 13, 14

S

salt pans (Gozo) 64
St George's 66
St Julian's 52, 66, 72–3
St Paul's Bay 50, 66, 73
St Thomas Bay 45, 46
San Anton Palace 36
San Blas Bay (Gozo) 60
Sannat (Gozo) 64
Sceberras Mount 13
Selmun Palace 50
Senglea 12, 27, 35, 39–41, 67
Sicily 10, 11, 16, 54
Sliema 25, 34, 52, 66, 67, 72
Spanish Aragonese 11, 17, 54
Suleiman the Magnificent, Sultan 11, 12
Syria 10

T, U

Ta'Cenc (Gozo) 64, 66
Ta'Dbiegi 69
Ta'Hagrat 17
Ta'Pinu (Gozo) 62
Ta'Qali 37, 68
Ta'Xbiex 67
Tarxien 17, 22
theatre 24
Three Cities 39–43, 67
Tigne Point 25, 35
Tunisia 21
Turks 11, 12, 54
Urban VIII, Pope 38

V

Valletta 13, 14, 17, 20–9, 71–2
  Palace of the Knights 23
  Piazza Indipendza 26
  St John's Co-Cathedral 22
  War Museum 27, 67, 68, 69, 76
Vasse, Giorgio Grognet de 38
Verdala Palace 48
Verdale, Grand Master Hugues Louvenx de 48
Victoria (Gozo) 55–9, 66, 69, 74
  Cathedral 57, 69
  Citadel 57
Victoria, Queen 23
Vilhena, Grand Master Manoel de 24, 32
Vittoriosa 12, 13, 22, 27, 31, 39, 41–3, 67

W–Z

White Tower 51
Wignascourt, Grand Master Aloph de 24
wines 75
Xaghra (Gozo) 59, 75
Xewkija (Gozo) 64
Xlendi (Gozo) 54, 64, 66
Zebbug (Gozo) 62

Art & Photo Credits

Photography	Lyle Lawson, and:
Front cover	Steve Bly/Tony Stone Images
Back cover	Glyn Genin
Handwriting	V Barl
Cover Design	Tanvir Virdee
Cartography	Berndtson & Berndtson

NOTES